What I Have Learned From My Six Sons

By
Jim Britt

What I have Learned from My Six Sons

Jim Britt

All Rights Reserved
Copyright 2019

High Serenity Retreat, LLC
10556 Combie Road, Suite 6205
Auburn, CA 95602

The use of any part of this publication, whether reproduced, stored in any retrieval system or transmitted in any forms or by any means, electronic or otherwise, without the prior written consent of the publisher, is an infringement of copyright law.

Jim Britt
What I have Learned from My Six Sons
ISBN (978-1-63227-264-5)
ISBN (978-1-63227-265-2)

Dedication

This book is dedicated to my wife Joanna and to my six sons Jeff, Jim, Warren, Weston, Will and Walker. Without them there would not have been a story to tell or a life full of meaning.

Table of Contents

Introduction: ix

Chapter One: Happiness is a Gift You Give Yourself 1
Don't pray for more things, but for wisdom and knowledge so that you might know what to do with all the things you've already been given.

Chapter Two: You are What You Honor Most 21
In order to awaken to our true greatness we must first suspect that a part of us is asleep. Awakening begins with self-observation.

Chapter Three: Re-Source-ful 46
Create your vision of what you want in life, then play with whomever shows up to play.

Chapter Four: Happiness is not in the Past or Future 77
Everyone is searching for the correct path to truth, while the real truth is, there is no correct path, except the one we create ourselves.

Chapter Five: With Death Comes the Recognition of Life 99
If we want to see how well we've done in our lives, all we need to do is watch our children. They are our greatest success.

Chapter Six: You Can Change Your Story 117
Don't let your experiences from the past dictate how you live your life in the present. The past is simply a memory, it doesn't exist in real life.

Chapter Seven: The Power of Imagination 141

If we focus on our inner harmony, our personality will reflect a certain peace that can only come from knowing our own inner spirit.

Chapter Eight: I heard the Voice of a Three Year Old Calling 162

The sadness is not to have died, the sadness is not to have achieved all that was within us to achieve while we lived.

Chapter Nine: The Power of Love 186

All I may achieve in the eyes of men means nothing if I have achieved nothing in the eyes of a child.

Chapter Ten: Freedom requires Responsibility 211

Lift your thoughts as high as the eagle lifts its wings so you may sour above the storm. For what we believe, we are

Epilogue: 236

Introduction

In his book, *Rings of Truth,* Jim Britt (portrayed as Matt) promised the reader a story that would invigorate the mind, open the heart and touch the soul. The book had, by all standards, done just that and in its success had touched the lives of all who have read it, in spite of Cindy's predictions. Cindy, his agent at the time he decided to write the book, was totally against it. But Jim knew in his heart it had to be written. He took a chance that people would want to read a book that opens the invisible door, steps into the personal life and reveals the truth that lies within.

He wanted the world to meet Michael and Alea, two beings, one a fictional character, (you'll have to decide which is real and which is fictional) who took him on a journey of self-discovery and personal change that touched every area of his life. They both entered his life as if at an appointed time and allowed him the joy of their strength as they instructed him and gave his life new meaning.

Because of the awareness they captured in his soul, Jim's thirst to identify and re-define his existence could not be quenched until it was expressed on paper and published.

The true source of his learning was not meant to be locked away for fear of critical review, but to be revealed to those who would open the pages, study them and then arrange the ideas according to their own truths.

Cindy had said the book would fail because he was displaying his emptiness, but instead the book was a success because he had shared his fullness.

It has been eighteen years since the final chapter of *Rings of Truth,* and, today as Jim looked back, he could see the gift of his decision, and he knew in writing the book, he had opened the hearts of the thousands who read it. It is an inspired book full of truth, he knew that and he was grateful to have listened to his heart.

The last chapter, however, was only the beginning. So much has happened since that day in Joshua Tree National Park and the lives of those in his story have gone on.

Reflecting back to the years prior to writing Rings of Truth, Jim's oldest son, Jeff, was a senior in high school then, and concerned that he make the right decisions about going into an unknown future. Later on a college graduate and today a successful computer programmer in Portland, Oregon.

Jim, the younger of the first two sons was playing little league baseball. Later, he extended his interests to track and field, broke the high school record in high jump, awarded a college scholarship, went on to college, got a degree in computer science and is now living in Seattle Washington.

Nan and Steve are married now and are very successful in their own careers, and Daryl has retired. Though time and space now separates Jim from them and contact is infrequent, the feeling of a close friendship is still shared and will always be remembered.

Jim, portrayed in Rings of Truth by Matt and Joanna Jim's wife, portrayed by Jessie now are the parents of four sons; Warren, Weston, Will, and Walker. They are all grown and having families of their own.

The one thing, however, that has remained constant is that Jim is continually rediscovering the truths. In the absence of Alea and Michael, his children have become his mentors in reminding him that all things of value are already known to us for they exist within our conscience. He has learned that as we walk with our children, they become our guides in that journey of rediscovery and the story continues...

Chapter One

Remembering back to a time when Warren was sixteen years old, Weston, twelve, Will, eight and Walker, six. I sat, looking at my cluttered desk. I felt a smile cross my face as I remembered that at one time I actually thought if I had a bigger desk there would be a place for everything. The clutter before me, however, proved that theory wrong for there was no end to clips, papers, pencils, and books, some open, some closed. The computer, its bright screen glaring, occupied the right side while the telephone took charge of he left. A calendar, the thought for today etched across the bottom of its page, tilted slightly toward the center as if competing with my favorite family portrait for the coveted spot. The picture, however, stood solid and refused to give way to intimidation. Add the calculator and every inch of available space was taken on the 4'x6' surface ironically called a desk top, since the desk top always seems to be on the bottom.

As my brain absorbed the scene in front of me I began to see the clutter on the desk from a different perspective and realized that within this scene was a new discovery waiting in the wings. I focused on the desk for several minutes just letting the truth unfold itself to me and slowly it began to conceive within my mind.

Life can present itself as a cluttered desk. We have all we need in front of us to complete ourselves but until we use the clip to hold something of value, until we push the 'on' button or dial outside our own little space, or until we remove yesterday from our calendar and work with today then all we have is clutter. Our books may be open and full of knowledge but until we know what to do with what we have learned or until we organize it and put it where it belongs the size of the desk will make no difference. In all the clutter we will have lost that for which we are really searching. We will have lost the picture, and when we lose the picture, we are lost.

Could there yet be another truth? No matter how cluttered our lives may become, as long as we keep what really matters in the center and we focus on that to bring us the happiness we seek, the clutter becomes irrelevant and we are content because we understand that clutter is just a part of life.

Interesting, truth in contrast from a cluttered desk, I thought to myself as I began to examine the conclusion. The conception would be determined by a frame of mind or perhaps, a learned analogy. Either one would be correct, however, and the result would be the same.

With a clear conscience I was now able to ignore the clutter and using the back of my chair for a pillow, I closed my eyes and let my mind drift back to yesterday and into the past. Yesterday, because it was the seventeenth anniversary of one of the most important days in my life, and the past because it has made me who I am today.

I shifted into a dream as the face of a beautiful woman whose radiant smile penetrates my very being, came into view. The softness of her blond hair complimented the hazel in her eyes, revealing their beauty. In her hands she held a bouquet of roses. On the third finger of her left hand, the ring that bonded our love glistened in the sun.

Thirty one years ago we made a commitment to dedicate our lives to each other and to love each other beyond anything else. In the years since that day I have discovered that love is really a way of life. It has to be or we are nothing. Love governs life. Love excites life and brings it into a full circle.

I hadn't realized how far we had come in our love until our fifteenth anniversary when I decided to have an art piece made for her.

The woman who was creating the canvas called to explain what she needed in order to do the painting and then said, "Ask your wife what is her most meaningful word. Then I also need to know what word is the most meaningful to you because I am going to work the two words and the definition into the painting. Just remember one thing, they can't be the same word."

My answer was already waiting for her as she finished. "Mine is love." I said, "I'll ask Joanna and then call you right back."

I didn't want Joanna to know what I was doing so as I walked into the room to ask my question I tried to be very casual. I smiled and commented on how lovely the flowers looked that she was arranging, then asked, as if the thought had just entered my mind, "What is the most meaningful word to you in the English language?"

Without looking up she answered, "Love."

It hadn't entered my mind that she might possibly choose the same word and I wanted to say, "No, you can't have that one," but caught myself in time and commented with, "Oh, ok." To which she responded, "Why do you want to know?" "Oh, no reason." I shrugged and smiled, then, with that information I hurried back to my office, called the woman and explained, "My word is love but so is my wife's."

Without hesitation she replied, "Ok, so what's your second most meaningful word?"

"That's not fair, she gets love and I don't?"

"Not at all, just ask her what her second most meaningful word is and tell me yours. I've had this happen before."

"Mine would be *integrity*." I answered before putting her on hold and hurrying off to ask Joanna.

"Mmm, I think it's *integrity*." This time she took a moment to look up. " Why are you asking these word things?"

"I'm doing this little survey," I lied. This was getting much more complicated than I had planned. Next year I buy her perfume.

As I made my way to the phone for the third time I had my third word in mind because I knew I would need one. "My third most meaningful word," I said into the receiver, "is *intimacy.*" I laughed as I explained that both Joanna and I shared the same word again. I shrugged my shoulders and sighed, "I'll call you back."

Once more I confront Joanna. "What's your third most meaningful word?"

She turned to me this time, tilting her face up so she could look me straight in the eye. Although her hair had been pulled back away from her face, several curled strands had managed to escape and, in doing so, had encircled her face, giving her an angelic look in spite of the frown she was now displaying. "What is it you are doing?" she demanded.

As much as I enjoy looking into Joanna's beautiful eyes, right now was not a good time. I'd heard once that the eyes cannot lie and I felt mine already shifting in preparation for the little white one I was about to tell so at the last minute I switched to the simple truth. "It's a surprise."

Her eyes held mine for a second longer then she whispered, "Intimacy." She touched my lips with her fingers, letting them linger there just long enough then turned and went back to her own project. She always did have perfect timing. I was in love all over again

As I made my way back to my office and the phone I thought of the love Joanna had shared with me through a simple gesture. It lasted only a moment but the memory lingered and as I picked up the phone and dialed a number I now have memorized I find myself whistling, and I'm whistling because someone shared their love.

What if all the problems in the world were handled with love? One government agent hands another government agent a file to view and instead of having CONFIDENTIAL or TOP SECRET, in big red letters, stamped across the front, it has HANDLE WITH LOVE. SHARE WITH EVERYONE, I wonder how many wars would actually be fought or how much hunger and crime there would be if everything were handled with love?

Love is a powerful force. Love spreads so fast that it's already everywhere at once. Love is power. In fact, it is the only true power. You can't even say the word without feeling the presence of it.

I heard the, now familiar, *hello* on the other end of the line so I had to put my thoughts about love on hold for a few minutes.

"Can you do this painting with intimacy for both of us?" I asked.

"Yes, I suppose I can," she replied, "but I need two different definitions, shall I hold?"

"If you don't mind, I'll only be a minute," I answered.

"Intimacy to me," she said, "is sharing your inner most feelings with another person."

"I like your definition," I said with relief, and hurried back to the phone.

"I think we have lift off," I laughed into the receiver. After repeating Joanna's definition to her, I gave her my own.

"Intimacy, to me," I explained, "is sharing the full experience of the moment."

"Two excellent definitions to work with," the woman on the other end replied. "They will make a divine painting.

As I hung up the phone I thought how intimacy doesn't necessarily have to involve another person. You can be intimate with a tree or a flower...or, for that matter, you can feel an intimacy in just being alone, sharing the moment with no one but yourself. However, intimacy, at this moment meant sharing with Joanna and I liked that feeling.

The painting was created. The definition of intimacy was woven in two different languages. The painting was in perfect harmony with the word from which it was created.

I felt a kiss, soft as a gentle breeze, brush my lips and a voice whispered in my ear, "I can see you are working very hard."

No one could dream a kiss like that nor the familiar scent of delicate perfume. I inhaled deeply, intoxicated by the fragrance and enjoyed the moment before opening my eyes to the woman in my dream.

"I thought you might be hungry," she smiled as she set a plate of sandwiches and an apple, neatly sliced into bite-sized pieces, on my lap. "I'm afraid that is the only empty space," she winked and nodded toward the desk.

My mouth watered as I picked up my favorite sandwich. Avocado, sprouts, tomatoes, cucumbers and cream cheese laced with mayo on 7-grain bread. I decided, yes, I was hungry and enjoyed one bite before expressing my appreciation.

"Thank you," I said after I swallowed. "It is delicious."

A smile spread across Joanna's face. "Were you meditating or just taking in air to pass the time?"

"Actually I was thinking about you. I don't think the love I feel for you can be expressed on canvas."

Joanna took a moment to absorb what I had said before answering. "It is my turn to say thank you." She pushed a few books around on the desk to clear a space then sat letting her slim legs dangle in the air. "Go on."

"Do you think love can be expressed on canvas?" I asked.

I watched Joanna's brows furrow as she looked at me for several seconds before responding. "I'm not sure what you mean."

"I've tried to envision a painting using our first most meaningful word, *Love*." I continued. "I asked myself, are there, on this earth, colors brilliant enough to paint the true beauty of love? What design could express its power? Even the most eloquent words known to man could not define its intention."

"I'm beginning to see what you mean. The beauty of love cannot be seen in a painting for the beauty lies in the giving for that is where the power lies," she expressed softly. "I know the love I feel for you can only be expressed in the giving. Sometimes the beauty of love is in something as simple as a sandwich. Another time the expression of love is in the birth of a child or the death of a loved one."

We sat there for several minutes just enjoying the presence of each other, then Joanna continued. "And now I will express my love by leaving and letting you get back to your work." She slid off the desk, took one of my apple pieces, kissed my forehead and left as silently as she had come. As she closed the door her essence of love lingered.

When had I first embraced this truth of love? A memory enveloped me and a name I held deep in my heart began to open the past as if it were a gate. Alea, who I can only explain as a spiritual guardian, not a physical being, had entered my life years ago and introduced the truth to me. She had taught me to look inside myself for that which is real and I had found it. She instructed me to look beyond the surface and to reach for the purpose just as I had done with the desk and the canvas. I smiled. She had taught me well.

I hadn't thought of Alea for some time now. I wonder if she still plays a part in my life in a physical sense or has she left me on my own with only her influence to guide me. I only know I haven't felt her presence for a very long time. What was it she had said to me?

"There will come a day when you no longer see me at all. What is important is that you feel me with you; this is what truly matters. There will even come a day when you are no longer aware of feeling me; it will just be a natural state of being."

The golden rings, evidence that she was real, have been carefully placed in a deep navy blue and turquoise velvet box, the colors of the water that surrounded the beach of Napali Coast in Hawaii. A reminder not only of who helped me discover truth but also where I began my journey of discovery.

How many years had it been since I took the rings from their box? I can't remember but with my eyes closed I could see the setting inside the box perfectly. The ring of *Surrender* was placed in the center of the box. Then each ring of the "Seed of Seven" arranged around it, interlocking like a circular chain; *Live each Moment, Self-observation, Courage, You are God and I am You, Let Go, I am not My Ego*.

Around the outside of the "seed", and the first seven rings, was a larger ring, Resourcefulness, completing the "seed of life". The remaining rings, each one overlapping and bisecting the next, created another circular chain pattern. *Clarity, Follow Your Heart,*

Commitment, Intimacy, Acceptance, Compassion, Integrity, Appreciation, Accept a Miracle, Give and Receive, Balance and Harmony. The ring *Responsibility*, almost completed the pattern as its size allowed it to encircle all the rings leaving one spot in the velvet box for the largest ring, the ring of *Love*.

I felt the unity in these truths as they flooded my soul. Just as the rings when linked in their pattern became a Master's key, the truth, when linked together became a masterpiece.

In order to become complete within myself, I had to be able to surrender those things that were without meaning. I had to let go of yesterday and live in the present. I had to have the courage to look inside myself and know who I am without my ego. I had to accept that I could let go of the pain that sustained that ego. Only then could I allow to flow within myself the integrity, the compassion, and the commitment I needed to follow my heart with clarity and to accept the miracle of the gift that had been given me, the gift of responsibility. I had to know the value of giving and receiving in order to take full responsibility. I needed to fully understand resourcefulness in order to bring balance and harmony, not only into my life, but into the lives of those around me. And I could do none of this without the capacity to love.

Just as each of the twenty-one rings in the box represent a truth the largest ring completes the pattern as it is placed on the outside of the last ring and encompasses all the rings and truths into a never ending circle of love.

I felt an overwhelming sense of gratitude and in my mind I carefully closed the velvet box and set it back into its hiding place and allowed myself to open my eyes. I gazed out the window knowing I was just beginning to comprehend the truths each ring represented. I had so much yet to discover, not so much in the outside world around me but the world that existed inside me.

I shifted perspective once again and spent the next few minutes studying the picture of my four youngest sons when they were youngsters. A fifteen-year old picture but still my favorite. Four handsome blondes dressed in identical red shirts. Warren, looking wise beyond his sixteen years, was holding Walker, the youngest, protectively on his lap while Weston, ten, and Will, six, stood close beside them. The picture had captured time and time could not separate them as long as they stood together.

As I examined each face their intelligent eyes seemed to focus on me. I stood and walked to the left of the desk. Their eyes followed. I shifted to the right of the desk. Their eyes followed. Inhaling deeply I felt a quiet peace settle over me and I smiled to myself as a thought came into my mind. Neatly encased in that beautiful oak frame were my own personal guardians.

I returned to my chair and studied their smiles. What each child held in his heart displayed itself in his smile. Each smile so different and yet so much the same. They didn't seem to mind the clutter surrounding them on the desk as long as I was sitting in front of it. I suddenly felt humble in their presence.

Questions presented themselves without consent in my mind and I began to do a little self-observation. How have I influenced my sons by the way I live? How do they see me? What do they see when they look into my eyes? Can they read my smile as plainly as I can read theirs?

At times I have just sat and watched them at play and absorbed the joy I felt for what I have. I wonder what they feel when they watch me at work? Do they feel joy in my presence? What would I see if I were able to view myself through my children's eyes? What is it like to have me as a father?

These are questions for which I'm not sure I want to hear the answers. No, that's not right. These are questions for which I need answers. Where do I find them?

As if on Qu the answer presented itself with a knock on my door.

"Dad," I heard Warren say as the door opened. "Need some quick advice."

"Isn't that interesting," I responded, "I need some quick advice too. There's a clean spot on the desk, have a seat."

Looking at me then at the desk, he nodded, and made his way to the spot Joanna had cleared a short time ago. Once he settled his slim, almost six-foot frame comfortably on the desk, he cocked his head slightly to one side, raised his left eyebrow and smiled my smile. "Now, what can I do for you?"

Almost instantly I could see myself in my sixteen-year old son. And I knew all I need to do to find the answers to my questions is to be with him.

"Ok, here's the question," I replied. "On a scale of one to ten how would I rate as a father?"

"You're limiting your abilities as a father, Dad, when you limit the size of the scale." He laughed then his face became serious and his eyes searched mine. "There is no scale, only me and Will and Walker and Weston. We are what we see in you and Mom."

A smile formed around his mouth, "It's like looking in the mirror when you look at me. Tell me, do you like what you see?"

I was startled for a second with his response, then, I realized I already knew the answer to my question, my son just had to remind me.

"As a matter of fact, Warren, I like very much what I see. I'm just wondering how much of what I see is your mother and how much is me," I chuckled. "Now, how can I help you?"

"Tell me, Dad," his eyes grew serious, "does pleasure and happiness mean the same thing or are they different? When I looked them up in the dictionary, their definitions were basically the same, but when I look around me what I see contradicts the definitions."

"I think that we, as human beings, have become quite skilled at confusing the two," I replied. "Give me an example."

"Ok, for example, some of the kids at school seem to take a lot of pleasure in using heroin or cocaine. But, in spite of all the pleasure they claim it gives them, they are never happy. As soon as the ecstasy of the high wears off , they become depressed and empty again. Yet, they never seem to look beyond the drugs or alcohol for what I think they are really searching for and that is happiness. They just want to be happy, don't you think, Dad?"

Warren was really struggling to understand what he was feeling, so choosing my words carefully I began to explain, "Often people confuse pleasure with happiness, and, on the surface they may seem one in the same, but what brings us pleasure may not ultimately bring us happiness. Happiness that depends on physical pleasure is unstable; one moment it's there and the next moment it's gone. We may recognize it in a kiss, a smile or a touch, or feel it in the warmth of the sun or in the beauty of a sunset. Many also know the pleasure of the ecstasy of a heroin high, a cocaine rush or an alcohol buzz..."

"I like the idea of a sugar zap from that second piece of Mom's pie, better." Warren interrupted with a smile.

"Or the 'chocolate charge' from a double-decker hot fudge sundae," I laughed.

"Try the 'power punch' of the newest energy drink," Weston chimed in from the doorway, holding the drink in front of him. His damp hair laid flat against his forehead where his ball cap had been. His face was slightly flushed and beads of sweat were still glistening on his upper lip. His running shoes were flung over his shoulder leaving a smudge on his tank top. It was obvious that he had just finished baseball practice. "What are we discussing, anyway?"

"You look like a walking advertisement for that drink you are holding in your hand," Warren remarked as he reached for the bottle to have a taste. "The question is this, are you drinking that for pleasure?"

"Pleasure? No. Energy? Yes," replied Weston as he handed the bottle to Warren. "Take a taste and, in one word or less, give me your opinion."

Warren lifted the bottle to his lips and, with reservation, took a small sip. "Yuck!" he exclaimed as he scrunched his nose and shuttered.

"Mmmm, I'm not sure that qualifies as a word. What do you think, Dad?" Weston laughed as he turned to his brother. "To tart for your taste, is it?

"If all those things we like to eat, that aren't good for us, tasted this bad, we'd be happy to stay away from them." Warren remarked.

"Excellent point," I seized the moment. "For pleasure we rely on outside influences. For happiness we have to rely on ourselves. If we could simply identify the substances we put into our mouths by their taste, then get rid of those that are harmful to our bodies and cultivate the good ones, how easy it would be to make sound choices that would bring us happiness.

The same is true when you talk about the mind. When there are thoughts that are harmful, we should strive to reduce them, and those that are constructive, we should nourish."

"That would work for destructive emotions too," Weston added. "If we really want to be happy, then we should eliminate anything that does not make us happy, then create those things that bring us happiness, right?"

"That's correct," I continued. "Not only are destructive emotions harmful to ourselves and keep us from our own happiness, but they are harmful to our relationships to our family, to society, and to the whole world."

Warren, who had been listening intently, responded, "The final consensus here, as I see it, is that happiness is a universal concept, and before we try the drugs or allow certain thoughts to enter our mind, or let our emotions control us, we need to ask ourselves, 'will this bring me happiness?' It's alright to have pleasure, unless we are seeking pleasure to find happiness or to hide the pain of our unhappiness."

He slid off the desk and offered me a taste of the sports drink, which I wisely refused, before going on. "I think there is a lot of pain behind the use of drugs. Kids think drugs or alcohol will make them happy, but they are wrong. If they could only see that to be in control of their lives and their futures, they just have to rescue the secret that is literally held prisoner within their own beings by the influence of the drugs that affects not only their bodies but also their minds."

"There is a natural law," I said, "that never fails, the law of 'Cause and Effect'. If you apply it a million times it works the same way every time. So, for example, if there is a certain event you don't want to happen, the best method of insuring it doesn't take place is to make sure the condition that caused the event doesn't happen. Similarly, if you want a certain experience to occur, the logical conclusion is to seek to create the cause and conditions that bring it forth."

"So how do you make them understand, Dad?" Warren asked. "How do we get the message out there?"

"That's a very good question, Warren," I replied, "Maybe all you can do is just be who you are around those who have yet to learn the concept. Keep the door to your heart open so you can communicate with them without judging. If you are strong in your conviction and still have the compassion toward those who are not, you can make a difference."

His eyes met mine as I spoke, and they revealed the doubt he felt inside that this could actually work.

"If you will do this," I explained, " you will be sending a message that you care how they feel in your presence, and that you can love and accept the person without accepting the act. If you can create a feeling of trust and resourcefulness, and they can feel your spirit of friendship and love, and if one person's life is changed because of you, then you have truly made a difference in the world."

"How can I feel compassion for them when they are deliberately destroying their lives?" Warren asked.

"What you don't realize is that you have already felt compassion because you have recognized their pain and you care enough to want to do something about it."

Genuine compassion is a state of mind that is based upon ones concern and respect for another human being...a wish for others to be free of their suffering. And you do this regardless of whether you view the other person as a friend or an enemy. You have already demonstrated that kind of compassion."

"I guess I have," he said as he allowed the thought to penetrate his mind. "Although I don't even know some of them, I still wish they could be happy without the need to look for happiness in the drugs and alcohol."

"That's right," I continued. "And now that you are aware of your compassion, do you think you can demonstrate it in the way we discussed?"

Weston and Warren nodded in agreement as Warren handed the bottle, still half full of energy drink, back to Weston.

"That's pretty powerful advice, Dad," Weston said before pausing to take a drink from the bottle. "I wish it was as easy as it sounds in this room. Here we have three guys who all think the same. Out there, life is pretty wild."

"Life wasn't meant to be easy, Weston," Warren winked. How fast or how far could you run if you didn't run every day? How hard you work at something determines how good you will be. You take it one mile at a time and you give it everything you've got or you give it nothing, it's up to you. You choose to give it everything you have and that's why you are so good. Life is the same. You have to work at it every day because life is what you make it. You give it all you've got or you give it nothing and life returns the favor. So what have you got to lose by going out there and just being Weston, Keeper of a Truth?"

Weston's eyebrows shot up in jest and Warren gave him a gentle poke in the ribs before continuing. "Happiness isn't just handed to us either, I suppose. We have to want to be happy bad enough to work at being happy every day too. Today, I choose to be happy."

With that he wrapped his arm around Weston's neck and gave him one of those brotherly half-nelson hugs and as they wrestled their way out of my office, Warren shouted back to be heard above Weston's complaints, "Thanks for taking the time to talk, Dad."

As they ducked and punched their way out the door I heard Weston laugh. "Hey, you don't have to take your happiness out on me. You better be careful or I'll happy you right back."

As their voices faded I thought to myself, "I hope I gave them good advice," I felt blessed to have sons who trusted me enough to ask my advice and yet I realized in giving advice I had to first listen, and in listening I had also learned from them.

The feeling of the moment seemed to surround me and only the need to finalize the material for my seminar inspired me to turn my attention back to my work. Leaning forward I reached for my folder of information but my hand refused to take instructions and I found I had instead, retrieved the first of many personal journals I had written in. Why it was on my desk, I will never know. But the need to rediscover its contents seemed to capture me and I found myself opening the book to the first page. The date was 1962, the year my first son was born. My eyes began to mist as my fingers touched the paper and I began to read silently the words...

I will never forget how I felt when I first held him in my arms. Not so much the fear but the pain of responsibility. I held him for several minutes just looking into his face, my heart pounding. Even the weight of this tiny baby seemed to overwhelm me and with tears rolling down my face I asked him, "Oh my son what do I do with you now?"

His clear little eyes looked up at me for a moment then he closed them. He yawned and stretched, and opened them again. He frowned at me as if pondering this question. Then I heard the words as plain as if he had spoken them himself. "Don't worry Dad, we'll do it together."

I felt an awakening in my heart as the words I had just read, pasted through my memory. With my first son I had discovered responsibility. But of even greater significance, I had discovered how it feels to love a child, and how it feels to have that love returned unconditionally.

WHAT I HAVE LEARNED FROM MY SIX SONS

I glanced at the books I had been studying and I knew with all the wisdom and knowledge I would find on their pages I would yet be left unfulfilled. What I am searching for is not found in books. What I am searching for can only be found in the eyes of my sons. It is there I will find the wisdom of the universe. I can only grow and discover through them as they grow and discover for themselves.

Just as no text can truly explain the feeling of love, no text can teach us what we already know. What is really important we already have written within us. It is a gift we are born with, all we have to do is remember who we really are. It seems as we grow older we tend to store away and forget the important stuff until our children bring those things back to life for us. By observing them, we can discover what we already know again and again.

I wonder if the part of my life that is written and will yet be written on the pages of my journals will make interesting reading. When my story is finished will it be filled with drama and excitement? Will there be humor along with the trials or laughter with the tears? Will my children know me better through the words I have written? Will the words that express the love I feel for them live in their hearts long after I am gone? Will my children's grandchildren read these journals, or other books I have written, one day, and embrace the truths I have discovered? Will they feel the love I have for them before I even know them?

I looked down at my journal once again and began to feel the power held within its cover. A power, warm and soothing, in my hands. How it found its way to my cluttered desk shall probably always remain a mystery. Why, when I was searching for material for a seminar, my hand was guided to a simple journal instead of books written by scholars, I may never be able to explain. But there is no doubt in my mind as to its purpose for being there.

Reflections

Journal Entry

The sun is setting and it is taking the pleasure of the light with it. Moving in slow motion it painted the clouds with a soft pink and silver, then began to wipe the colors with a touch of gold. Just as I was enwrapped in its beauty, it disappeared into the night. Appearing in its absence, stars began to fill the sky and as I watched I couldn't help but let the stress of the day fall away. What a gentle way for the sun to say goodnight.

The night air is cool and soothing and as I write in my journal I feel almost poetic and I'm thinking in simple lines instead of sentences. I think I'll just let it flow.

I reach back in time to a cluttered desk,
a smile, a tender touch, the whispered softness of a gentle voice.
The delicate fragrance of perfume.
These are things to remember.

A picture that does not change with time.
Faces of children, treasures of my soul,
My heart is full of love.
These are things eternal.

Our children are a reflection of ourselves,
keepers of the universe, teachers of wisdom,
messengers of truth.
These are things to write about.

WHAT I HAVE LEARNED FROM MY SIX SONS

Memories of Alea, who showed me the way,
whose influence guides me still.
Golden Rings of truth, a velvet box.
These are things never forgotten.

Pleasure and happiness are not one in the same.
Pleasure comes from others, a gift of the world,
Happiness comes from within, a gift you give yourself.
These are things to understand.

Knowledge is a gift born within us,
Unlimited, timeless, without condition,
Held there for us to nurture and discover.
These are things never ending.

Love is happiness, again and again,
Giving and receiving, sharing and forever present.
It is everywhere at once, yet cannot be explained.
This is a precious gift we are all born with.

The pages of a book filled with experiences both good and bad,
Both happy and sad, humor and trials, power and love,
And the simple words, Don t worry Dad, we'll do it together.
These are things that are priceless.

Thought for the Day

Don't pray for more things,
but for wisdom and knowledge
So that you might know what to do with all the things
you've already been given.

Chapter Two

The phone was ringing as I opened the door to my office. After completing the conversation with the gentleman on the other end, I sat down to consider the magnitude of what I had just been offered...an invitation to do a spiritual retreat in Peru. The thought of it sent chills through me because It was something I think I have wanted to do for a long time, but had never taken myself seriously. Why I would select Peru, I have no idea, but without provocation, it has consistently found its way into my thoughts. Now, today, the door has been opened to me. I just have to decide 'if' and 'when'.

I glanced at the calendar on my desk and noted that it had been a week since I had given my fatherly advice to Warren. I wish I could walk into my father's room right now and ask him what he thought of this opportunity.

Michael Angelo was once asked how he created such beautiful sculptures out of a piece of stone. He replied, *I simply hold a vision in my mind of what I want to create, and I chip away what doesn't support my desired outcome.*

I would hardly compare myself to a beautiful sculpture. I would only compare the process by which I have achieved the desired outcome. In the beginning I had to create a vision of how I wanted my own world to revolve then chip away at all learned behaviors and self-destructive beliefs that held it prisoner.

It is true that we create in our lives what we honor most. Whether it's our happiness, business success, financial gain or our relationship with another, what we focus upon, or honor is what we'll bring into our lives.

What we have in our future will always be based upon what we honor most in the present. And what we have in the present is totally based upon what we have honored in our past, nothing more, nothing less.

I thought of the young man I had met a few years ago at one of my seminars. He walked up to me as we were breaking for lunch and asked for my advice about a business he was thinking of starting.

"I know you have a lot of entrepreneurial business experience," he said, "and I would like to tell you about one I'm thinking of getting involved in."

I can't remember a time I haven't been interested in hearing about a new business adventure so I said I would be happy to help him in any way I could.

We walked outside where we could talk without interruption. It was a beautiful spring day and it matched the enthusiasm with which he told me, not only, about his new business venture and of his vision for its success, but what it would mean to him personally and financially. It was an exciting idea and I asked him when he planned to get started.

"Well," he began, "right now I'm going through a lot of *stuff* in my life that's holding me back. I'm going through a divorce which is taking a lot of my mental energy. I'm also going through an IRS audit that's really stressful. My company where I work may be downsizing and I could be one that gets cut..."

I finally interrupted, "Would you mind if I asked you a question?"

"Sure, go ahead," he answered.

"Which do you honor the most, your vision for success and the fulfillment that your success will bring you, or all the problems you shared with me...the *stuff* that is holding you back?"

He stood there for a moment with a puzzled look on his face. I'm sure he was thinking I hadn't really been listening.

"I honor my vision, of course," he said with passion.

"If that's true, then why let your stuff hold you back?"

"But you don't understand. I'm going through a divorce, I'm going through an audit and I may lose my job." He ran his fingers through his hair as he spoke and I could sense his frustration.

"There is one thing I do understand for sure," I said simply as I motioned him to a bench under the shade of a tree. "Life involves problems. Just as soon as you work through all your current problems, it will simply mean that you have worked through those problems, and you'll then have a whole new set that will take their place, and then you will have to deal with those problems. Life involves having problems. When you no longer have problems, you probably won't have a pulse. The reason that most people end up broke later in life is because they let their problems and fears run their lives. They honor their problems instead of their vision for a better life"

As we sat on that bench discussing life and business and how they are all part of the picture I explained that in order to create what we want in our lives, we must first let go of whatever it may be in our lives that is holding us back. I explained to him that it's not that we don't handle our problems, we just don't allow them to be our main focus in life. We handle each problem by looking at it as one of the things we need to resolve or let go of in order to move forward. Yes. You will have problems, but a problem is simply a signal that you have approached something incorrectly. Handle it, yes, but don't let it consume your vital energy and focus.

As we parted, he seemed much more confident and I wished him well. I believe that young man went on to face his future with renewed enthusiasm.

Our lives are not about the lessons we think we are here to learn. Our lives are about discovering who we really are while we are here. It's about uncovering our true nature. It's about waking up to who we are which requires letting go of that which we imagine ourselves to be.

Once we have discovered the pure self within our own being, only then can we forget *self* and go out into the world and help others. We cannot teach what we do not know ourselves. We cannot show others unless we know the way.

I hear so many people say things like "God has a plan for me," "God is putting me through this hardship to learn a lesson". The reality is that we all create our own plan and put ourselves through hardships and God will support you in whatever you decide to do.

We are all teachers and students. I had many teachers in my life. My parents who loved me enough to teach me how to work and yet allowed me to follow my own path.

My first son, Jeff, opened the door to what is real in my life and cemented my foundation. I only wish I had known more so I could have served him better. I would give anything if I could go back and teach him more about joy and what it meant to live your own truth.

Jim, who came along a few years later, arrived with a love for life. He demonstrated the will to live fully and an enthusiasm that had escaped me until I watched a young boy greet each day as a new beginning. Once the door was opened to this new life I had stepped into, Jim became my guide to new and exciting experiences. In his zest for living he introduced me to a world I hadn't known existed and taught me to live life more fully. I wish I had taken the time to be more of an intimate part of his life to discover, along with him, the excitement, fascination and rewards that life can hold.

I have found that we experience the world as we see it. The universe will always give us back an accurate reflection of our vision. What was it Warren had said? *We are what we see in you and Mom.* As I think about that I realize that statement could be taken even one step further, *we are what we see in ourselves.*

Right now to see myself was to read and review my life. Would I like what I read? For the most part I was handling life pretty well, I thought. Flaws are supposed to be part of a man's character. They keep us humble, I suppose, and I had been generous with myself in that department. There are still empty pages to be filled, however, and though perfection is beyond my grasp at least I'm moving forward learning and growing.

There was a simple way to find out. All I needed to do was pick one of several journals from the bookshelf and open its cover. I did just that. The year printed on the front of the cover was 1995. As I read I felt myself being transformed from simple reader to captivated student. The pages before me were filled with stories that had shaped and refined my life, and I was discovering myself once again. An entry dated March 10, 1995, brought back a special memory and I began to read.

As I watch Warren grow I realize that with his birth he brought a

level of simplicity. He believes that anything is possible and has the confidence to test the idea for himself. He's not afraid to try. He has the courage to just do it.

Several months ago he came into my office filled with excitement

over a video game he wanted to buy. The video game, however, carried a price tag of $118.00...

I smiled to myself as I read those first two paragraphs. Even though the book lay open on my lap, I didn't need to read anymore to recall the memory in full. I can still hear Warren's voice as he stood in the doorway of my office...

"It's a really neat video game, Dad. Will you buy it for me?" he asked as he leaned against the door frame of my office. I glanced up at him. He was tall for his ten years, his hair was hidden underneath his baseball cap. His shoes showed wear from games played by ten-year old boys. He looked healthy and happy. All in all I thought he could handle my answer.

"I don't think so," I replied.

He must have known I meant what I had said because he left the room without saying anymore. Pretty soon he was back, however, with a proposition.

"If I earn half the money, would you put up the other half?" he asked with determination and I could see he really wanted this game.

"Ok, I think that would work," I said and then waited for him to say more, but he simply nodded and started to leave the room again.

Then he stopped and turned to me, concern showing on his face, "What would you suggest I do to earn the $59.00?"

"That is something you will have to figure out for yourself, Warren." I smiled and he gave me a nod that spoke for itself and he was gone again.

I went back to my work and my son went to devise his business plans. Two hours later he walked back into the room carrying a Mrs. Field's Cookies recipe book and a brown paper sack.

"Have you ever tasted a Mrs. Field's cookie, Dad?" He asked.

"I think I've had a few," I answered, my mouth watering with the thought of the chocolate chip ones with macadamia nuts.

"Have you ever tasted one you didn't like?"

"Can't say that I have," I had to admit. "But then, I haven't tried all of them." When I thought of Mrs. Field's, I thought of the chocolate chip cookies with the macadamia nuts. I didn't know there were enough different kinds to fill a recipe book.

"Mrs. Field's cookies are huge, Dad." He demonstrated with his hands as he spoke, his face beaming with confidence. "But, you know what, I've gone through this book and found a recipe I like and I think I can make it even better. Mom said she would put the money up front for the ingredients and I'll pay her back out of my proceeds. I'm going to make the cookies better and I'm going to make them bigger than, I'm going to sell them for twenty-five cents more. They will be called *Mr. Britt's Cookies.*"

He held up the brown paper sack he had in his other hand. On the front of the bag he had laid out his design. A heart with "Mr. Britt's Cookies" in colorful letters carefully centered in the middle. He reached inside the sack and pulled out a sandwich bag.

"Each cookie will be put in one of these to keep it fresh for delivery because fresh cookies are the best," he remarked as he put the sandwich bag back into the sack.

He had thought of everything from the quality and size to the integrity of the product he would be selling. I looked at my son and I was impressed with what I saw. In front of me stood a young man full of confidence, ingenuity, purpose, and above all, integrity.

"How many cookies are you going to bake?" I asked, curious as to how he had planned for that.

"However many I sell." He went on to explain. "I will go around and take orders and get the money and then I'll bake the cookies and deliver them fresh that same day."

In my adult thinking I wondered if that would work. Would people actually give him an order and the money without seeing the cookie first? I was careful in my response to Warren's idea because how did I know it wouldn't work.

"You're going to sell them first and then bake them?"

He looked at me and smiled. "It's going to work, Dad," he said and off he went to start his "Mr. Britt's Cookies" business.

In the first two days, Warren had made $85.00. He first went around the neighborhood, just as he explained he would, describing the kind of cookie he was making. His customers placed their order. He collected the money, hurried home and baked the cookies, put them in the sandwich bags, inside the decorative brown paper sack, and while they were still warm made the deliveries.

I remember the day we were preparing to leave for the weekend and Warren had one cookie left to deliver. He asked if I would drive him to make this delivery because it was so far away. I agreed and off we went. We had driven almost two miles before stopping in front of his customer's home. While he took the cookie to the door, I couldn't help but wonder why he had come so far to sell one cookie.

He walked back to the car with a smile on his face. As he climbed into the car and shut the door, I asked, "Why the smile?"

"Because she likes my cookies," he replied. "That's why I come here."

I was curious as to why he hadn't sold his cookies closer to home. His answer was simple. "I stopped at all those houses too, but they didn't want any cookies today."

In the adult world I knew that sales people often times feel a great sense of rejection at the word "no". How many homes had he gone to that day and received a "no"? I was curious as to how he had handled the rejection he must have experienced so I asked, "Warren, when you called on all those houses and they told you 'no', what did you think?"

He turned to me with a puzzled look on his face and said, "I thought they didn't want a cookie and I said, 'thank you', and went to the next door. Why?"

"No reason," I replied, "just curious."

In his ingenuity he also quickly found that if he always looked his best and took his younger brother, Weston, with him when knocking on doors, the people were even more apt to order the cookies. Weston was cute and too young to lie. This gave credibility to the business.

One day while he was getting Weston ready to go out I asked, "How much are you paying Weston for his work?"

Warren looked at me quizzically and then replied, "Nothing. I hadn't thought about paying him. He thinks it's fun coming with me."

"I wonder how much of your business depends on him?" I inquired innocently.

Warren looked at the sacks that were lined up on the table ready for delivery. After calculating in his mind for a few minutes, he said, "I think I'll give him ten percent of the profits."

"That sounds fair to me," I replied as I opened the door for my entrepreneur and his assistant. Out they went, their arms full of sacks and the sacks full of cookies.

It was getting close to Halloween so Warren decided he would make Halloween cookies. The orders began pouring in and the pumpkin faced cookies started going out. He had an idea, while delivering the Halloween cookies, that people would probably want to order Thanksgiving cookies. He was right. As he delivered the Halloween cookies, orders were placed so when Thanksgiving came all he had to do was bake the cookies and deliver them to his already established clients. A very resourceful business move for the young entrepreneur, I thought.

Christmas was the big season and the orders were very profitable. Angels and Santa Clauses covered the table. Each one checked for perfection, then placed carefully in the sandwich bags and put into special Christmas Season, *Mr. Britt's Cookies* bags.

Super Bowl was next. Football cookies replaced the angels and Santa Clauses.

Warren's business had proved to be a success and the time had come to evaluate the future. He came into my office a week after the Super Bowl game and sat quietly in a chair facing me. He waited patiently until I finished doing whatever it was I was doing, then, in a very sober voice said, "I did it, Dad." A smile worked its way across his face in spite of his desire to control his excitement. "I have earned more than enough and I bought the game myself, although I will hold you to the deal we made, if you don't mind. You owe me $59.00".

"I think that is only fair," I responded. "So how is the cookie business going?"

"I closed my doors of business yesterday," he replied with a sigh of relief. "I think I have saturated the market with my cookies besides I have earned five times over what I set out to earn. I've decided that a wise businessman knows when it's time to fold the business. So, yesterday I baked my last batch of cookies and gave them to my customers, free of charge, and thanked them for their business. Not bad, aye, Dad?"

He retrieved a small notebook from his pocket, opened the cover and handed the book to me to read. I was impressed not only at how much he had made but also by the way he had kept an account of his transactions.

"Warren," I said after looking over his accounts, "I believe you have mastered the business world. What are you going to do with the rest of the money you have earned?"

"Mom took me to the bank yesterday to set up a savings account then I brought home some information on investment plans," he answered, his eyes full of excitement and his smile full of confidence. "I think I'll use the money I earn from the interest to buy my first car. What do you think, Dad, about investing my money verses leaving it in a simple savings account?"

We sat for several minutes discussing money and then Warren's manner changed and he became very serious as he spoke, "I can't figure out why people can't make money. It seems to me that all you need to do is to find something people want or need and you provide it. In doing that you make money. It's so simple. But, you know, Dad, some of the kids I go to school with don't have anything because their parents don't have any money. Why is it that way? Why don't they know what to do?"

"Not everyone has your courage, Warren," I replied.

"What do you mean?" he asked.

"Many people get stuck in their outdated beliefs or their old habit patterns of doing things and don't have the courage to break out of their comfort zone. Most don't even stop to consider, or even suspect that there could be a better way."

"What's a comfort zone, Dad?"

"People become comfortable in the way they were taught as they were growing up," I explained. "It's what they know. Changing would mean taking a risk, challenging their old beliefs. That is very frightening and uncomfortable for many people, therefore, they choose to just get by."

"What are they afraid of?" he questioned.

"Fears like; 'what if my business doesn't work? What if the opportunity I'm becoming involved in isn't real? What if my products aren't accepted in the marketplace? What if I can't do it? For some it can even be the fear of success."

"Ah come on Dad, you're joking. Everyone likes success." Warren looked at me in disbelief.

"As strange as it may seem, Warren, some people are very afraid of their own success. They may think; If I'm successful I may have to leave some of my friends behind, or, I may have to stretch to learn some new skills. To some the fear is taking on more responsibility."

"Do you mean that people decide for themselves how successful they are going to be without even knowing it?"

Warren lifted himself out of the chair and walked over to the window.

He stood, looking out in silence for a moment then spoke. "Maybe it's like me, standing here looking through the window, and out there I can see a whole bunch of great stuff I could do to make lots more money than I did with the cookies. But, I can't get out there to do them because of this barricade of glass. I know if I break it I can just walk out there and do what I want. But, if I break it I also know that you will make me pay for another window and that would take all the money I made selling cookies. So I have to decide if I have enough courage to take the risk of breaking the window and using not only the money I was going to buy my video game with, but also the money I was going to save for a car...."

He paused then and turned around to face me, a big smile on his face and a mischievous glint in his eye. "You know something? I think I'd still break the glass in spite of the consequences, because out there I see Britt's Landscaping company instead of Britt's Cookies."

"Good example," I said. "But remember that even though you have the courage to break through, you can't just walk out there and take what you want without a plan that will build Britt's Landscaping Company. You have to prepare yourself first. It's an ongoing process of personal development and without the plan you will find yourself back behind the glass. A person's success in life will never far outgrow their own development. Maybe that is one of the greatest fears. But as you face your fears and overcome them you also grow in confidence in return.

People sabotage themselves with their own self-imposed limitations or beliefs. When they break free of that limitation for a brief moment without a plan to change that belief, they simply sink back into their old ways."

"Kind of like watching a movie forward then hitting the 'rewind' button and watching it in reverse. I break the window, walk through but, no plan except to punch 'rewind" and, poof, back safely behind the glass.

Right!" Warren said as he reached over and picked up his notebook and closed the cover. "So, Dad, why was I so successful in my first business?"

"We develop our beliefs through the experiences we have in life, Warren," I explained. "You had no experience in business, therefore, no beliefs about why it may not work. You didn't even need courage because you had no fear."

Warren put his notebook back into his pocket and walked back to the window before asking, "If you don't have fear, you don't need courage?"

"That's correct," I answered. "When you have no fear then courage becomes a natural act."

"Ok, how do people get rid of their fears especially if they don't know that they have fears in the first place? I mean, you can't get rid of something that you don't even know you have." Warren's question was perfect.

I left my chair and walked over to the window by Warren. Outside we could see spring. Blossoms were beginning to bud on the trees looking like little popcorn balls and the sun was conducting its spring symphony as birds fluttered around the blossoms doing what comes naturally.

I wonder why in this world of natural beauty, do we as humans spend so much time in an unnatural state of fear, and we don't even know it? I looked over at Warren who was nodding and realized I still hadn't answered his question. "Self-observation." I said.

"Huh?" He looked at me and furrowed his brows.

"In answer to your question. First you have to realize you are hanging on to fear in the first place and that it is stopping you from whatever it is you want in life."

"Ok, I can see that. Then what do you do about it once you've recognized it?" His face grew more serious now and I could tell he really wanted to know.

"There are three more things you need to do," I continued. After self-observation comes intention, then willingness and commitment. You have to make the decision to let go, then you have to be willing to let go. That's where courage is important. After that, you have to make a commitment to let go and move to the next level of your development to break out of your comfort zone, to leave the old you behind. Then you simply let go."

"I think I understand," he said quietly.

We sat in the stillness of the room not saying anything while he pondered our conversation, his past few months in his business and what he had accomplished, and I watched a quiet transformation from little boy to young man take place.

My memory hadn't forgotten the details of that experience but I wanted to read the words I had written at the end of the entry, so I turned my attention back to the journal and read the last few paragraphs...

In the room I could sense a feeling of harmony and balance.

Things were as they should be. I will miss the little boy that was now gone but I shall honor the young man who took his place.

Warren stood then and reaching across my desk, shook my hand.

"Thanks Dad. Thanks for being here." He walked to the door.

Then paused and turned slightly. "I'm going to buy the game tomorrow afternoon after school." He winked and left the room.

It is the best $59.00 I have ever invested.

I closed the book and sat quietly in contemplation as the words, *Thanks, Dad, for being here,* spiraled through my mind.

I had watched as Warren outlined and operated his business. I watched as he carefully made his cookies as perfect as a ten year old can make a cookie. I watched as he ran off to deliver the cookies while they were still warm because freshness of the cookie was his calling card.

I was impressed that he was content to wait until the money was earned before buying the tape. In fact, he seemed in no hurry as his account began to grow. It was not until everything was added up and deposited that he finally made his purchase.

No, I thought, *thank you Warren. Thank you for being here.*

I reached for a piece of paper and a pen and I wrote all the things I had learned from my son during those months. At the top of the page I wrote: *Warren's Teachings,* then I underlined the words to give them more meaning.

Warren's Teachings

1. To have the courage, to step out of the crowd, to be bold.
2. When you have no fear, courage then becomes a natural act.
3. To take a risk and to look for the opportunity in the risk instead of focusing on the risk in the opportunity
4. Without the risk you can neither have failure or success. You can only fall back into your comfort zone.
5. Anything is possible, you just have to make a firm decision, then go do it.
6. Integrity has to be a priority to be truly successful.
7. First impressions are important. Look your best. You can only expect what you give.
8. We are born with all the talents we need to be successful in any endeavor.
9. Success in life and business are really simple.
10. Don't take rejection personally, it's not about you, they just don't want a cookie right now.

As I read the list over again I realized that these are values I already use in my own life. I had just rediscovered them.

One thing Warren had yet to discover, however, was that sometimes things don't work out just as we planned, and if they don't it is because they are not supposed to, though we may not see that until later in our lives when we can look back with objectivity and can be thankful it didn't. Sometimes failure helps us slow down long enough to evaluate and then we can move on and get to where we want to be.

Perhaps that will be one of the great discoveries he will make one day and, though in my heart I didn't want him to experience failure at all, in my mind I knew he had to, for it was there he would find the creation of his character.

What else was it that Warren had said? *It's like looking in the mirror when you look at me. Tell me, do you like what you see?* What I saw was strength of character I hadn't achieved until I was much older. I saw clarity in the vision he had created for himself. Everything about his plan to sell cookies was clear and well thought out. He had the ability to follow his heart, which meant he trusted the messages and intuition he was receiving within himself.

I saw commitment, that extra resource that you draw upon when the going gets tough. He was able to clarify what he needed to succeed and then to follow through no matter how much work it required. And, at times, the work was hard and the going was tough in his ten-year old mind, especially if there was something else he wanted to do instead of make and deliver cookies.

But, most important, I saw integrity. He gave all of himself in his commitment and his customers recognized that in him or I doubt they would have ordered and paid for the cookies in advance.

It is true, what we are inside, we teach our children. They don't hear the words we speak, they hear the silent words expressed only in our actions.

In turn, if we as parents could hear the needs of our children by observing their behaviors, how much more loving and fulfilling would the parent/child relationship be? We are so busy being a parent, trying always to teach, that we forget to listen to our child so that we can learn.

What I could see in my son had I taught by just being? Was my example his teacher? I had taught a concept without even realizing it, and only through watching my son could I rediscover the philosophy I had used in my own life.

Hadn't Jeff done the same thing as a boy when he had started his own business raking the neighbor's yards? I remember he came to me and asked for a loan to buy the tools he needed. He said he would pay me back out of his profits, which he did within the first few months. His lawn raking business became very profitable.

Jim was only eight when he set up a route around the neighborhood and collected aluminum cans to pay half on a new mountain bike he wanted. I matched his profit and we bought a fine mountain bike.

A question took form in my thoughts. What if I had allowed my experiences to lead me along another path, what would I be teaching my sons today?

What if I had been too busy to take the small hand that reached out to me and had failed to listen to a little boy's voice when he said, *Come quick, Dad. Ya' gotta' see this.* What if I had not followed as he led the way into an adventure of the things that mattered most in his life? Would that little boy have bothered to learn from a father who was too busy to learn from a little boy?

I wonder if God keeps a journal and if he does would my name be found there? I felt a chuckle start to form inside. I tried to suppress it because I wanted to keep this idea on a reverent tone but the chuckle found its way out into the open as I was imagining the size of his journal. I think God has a sense of humor so he won't mind.

I tried to think of something He might write about me. Let's see... *Jim's road is a little rocky today and he stumbled, but he is learning to walk with more determination.*

I hope He would write... *Jim has learned that love comes from within. Courage and compassion are beginning to find their place in his heart.*

A later entry might read... *Today Jim decided to knock at my door. To his surprise he found the door was already open and he just had to walk in. There are no preliminaries.*

And, finally... *Jim no longer has to believe in me, he now understands the purpose and his belief has surrendered to a deep knowing in his heart that I am always here.*

I closed the journal I held on my lap and returned it to the shelf, and reached for the journal I knew held the answer. The entry was dated January 1994...

Will is a very quiet and spiritual three-year old. He speaks of being with God before and of going back to God. Even though he loves his mother and me, greater even is his love for God.

Through his personal relationship with God, he has been given a

gift, the ability to sense illness in another person, whether it is physical or emotional. With angelic innocence he will rub his hands together and walk over to that person and lay his hands on them. Then, in a tender, sweet voice he softly says, "I am healing you with God's energy."

Yesterday, I was sitting in my office and I heard the door being opened quietly and almost as silently I heard a whispered *hsst*. Without even looking up I knew who it was.

"What do you want, Will?" I asked quietly.

He whispered back, "Come here, I want to show you something. Don't make a sound."

I knew, in his mind, there had to be something important for me to see or he wouldn't be here so I got up and walked over to him. He slid the door open to the sunroom and took my finger and whispered again. "Don't make a sound. I've got to show you something, come with me."

We walked through the sunroom out onto the balcony and to the huge old oak tree at the end of the balcony. It's the middle of winter so there are no leaves anywhere.

He stopped and said in a voice so soft I could barely hear. "Look, Dad."

"What is it?" I asked.

He pointed. "Look, right there and over there and right there." His little fingers moving from one point to another as he spoke.

I kept looking, I wanted so badly to see what had made him glow with excitement. My eyes searched but all I could see were the effects of winter.

"Don't you see them, Dad?" He finally asked, his voice barely audible.

I'm searching for anything. A bird or a squirrel, any kind of animal but I can't see anything. I said, rather disappointed with myself, "No, I can't see anything."

"Look up where my arm is pointing," he whispered as he pulled me to my knees, his little arm raised at an angle stretching toward the leafless oak tree. "Do you see them now? They are right there." Then he moved his little finger to the right as he spoke, "and right there and right there!"

I looked at him and I asked quietly, "What do you see up there?"

"Angels, Dad. There are angels in our tree. There are three angels sitting right there in the tree, don't you see them? Look, right there."

I turned to the tree and then I turned back and looked at Will.

The sun had caught the blonde of his hair in its rays casting a halo effect around his chubby little face. His eyes sparkled in the sunlight and there I saw the angels, not in the tree but in my child's eyes. I saw them because I knew he saw them.

As I write this event in this book a chill runs through me. What if I had said I was too busy to come right now. I would have missed seeing the angels though the eyes of my son. Because I walked with him today, tomorrow I will see the angels for myself.

I closed the journal then. I didn't want anything to disturb the unexplainable emotion I was experiencing inside. It almost hurt it was so intense. I know that God looks down and sees us and knows our potential. And, if we will allow it, that power we hold within us will guide us and we will achieve our fullest potential, whatever that may be. Today I see angels.

Contrary to what we may think, we are not here to teach our

Children, but to learn from them. We are their role models, not to make them replicas of what we are or what we wish we had been, but their guides and their protectors. We are here to help them live their lives not decide their futures, only to open the way for them to discover their own dreams. It is not for us to program them with all the adult things that make us adults and cause them to lose that child-like enthusiasm for they do not belong to us, they belong to themselves.

Someone once said to me that they wished babies came with a set of instructions. Basically a "How To" book. The only problem is that children are not like computers. We can't just turn them on and off at our convenience. That's not the way it works. There are, however, if we listen closely, instructions written inside our hearts and minds. They say, *watch your child while he plays, listen to your child when he speaks, and when he says,* "*Dad come and see the angels or, hurry Dad, I need you.* If we follow these simple instructions we have all we need.

I glanced at the clock. Several hours had passed since I received the phone call that had triggered the memories that took me on an adventure through my journals. It had been my intention to put ideas together for the seminar I'm presenting on Thursday when I stepped into the office. I gathered up the notes I had written yesterday and found nothing useful. It was what happened after I unlocked the door to my office today. Life happened. It got in the way and presented me with a wealth of information like a tiny miracle. Yesterday, I was sitting at my desk stuck in neutral. Today, real-life events began weaving their way in, and like little keys began to unlock thoughts and feelings and everything started to fall into place.

What was that phrase I like so well?

He who looks outside, dreams.

He who looks inside awakes.

In my awakening I was given a deeper understanding of what I know. And, as if inspired, another name came into my thoughts. Michael, my mentor and my friend, whom I have not seen in over seventeen years, yet who guides me still through the power of his words. Simple words, really, not eloquent by the standards of scholars, but words that span the universe and never lose their meaning.

He spoke to me, one day, of my awakening and my purpose. He told me that I had volunteered to help others reach enlightenment. Where and when I had volunteered I'm still trying to imagine, but when he spoke those words my heart leaped and I knew he had spoken the truth.

Michael was a man, or rather an angel of profound insight and every time he spoke his words seemed to leave indelible imprints in my mind and heart. We had spoken often during my years of awakening and he always left me with a feeling of renewal.

One day, as we talked of my responsibility, he said to me, *teach the people that we are all made up of the same divine stuff, and when we help another, we help ourselves. When we help ourselves from a centered place, we help all the beings of the planet.*

Imagine that when you die you review your life with total unconditional love surrounding you, keeping you safe. Then imagine that, at that time, you don't experience your life from your viewpoint, but rather you relive the experience that others had as a result of knowing you or resulting from your actions. In other words, you feel what they felt on account of you.

I thought about the people to whom I would be speaking. Would their lives be better as a result of something I might say or do? Would my life be better because of them?

I could hear Michael's voice echoing in my ear, *"remember you are not just teaching material, you are influencing human beings."* I smiled as I considered those words and I wished, within my heart, that I could turn around and Michael would be standing there, dressed in the same blue overalls and red plaid shirt he was wearing the first day I met him. The old felt hat sitting comfortably on his head, and his bright intelligent eyes looking straight through me as he smiled back. Maybe he is somewhere close by, making sure I stay awake.

I think Michael would approve of my trip to Peru, and I think Joanna will approve when I discuss it with her.

I thought about the day and what I had felt and experienced. I thought of the words I had written in my journal about the cookies and the angels and how Warren and Will had taken me on a journey into a world of exciting discovery. I recalled the words that struck my heart with tenderness, *Thanks, Dad, for being here*, and I felt safe in the total and unconditional love the author of those words expressed to me. I thought of God's journal and hoped that in review of my life He is, so far, pleased with me. I thought of the little hand that held mine and showed me the angels, and the mother of that child who holds my heart. These are the things I will take with me when I stand before that audience, not what I had written on paper.

I picked up a pen, then, to write in my journal. Tomorrow I will have lost the emotion of this moment and that emotion needed to be felt in the words that I wrote. The tears felt warm that came as the pen inked the page with a feeling that filled my heart and an awareness that filled my conscience. As I wrote I began to see the simplicity of it all. It's not the big things that happen in life but the simple things just happening each day that creates a world of wonder and beauty.

Our lives are about the special moments we experience. We don't really remember all of our past, only the meaningful as well as the unfortunate experiences we've had along the way. Those experiences, both good and bad, are what make us the person we are today.

Twenty minutes had passed before I finally closed the journal, and opened the top drawer to my desk to slip it inside. I moved aside several items already in the drawer to make a place for this precious book, then slowly I closed the drawer, watching as the book disappeared into the darkness. Another day I would take it out and read again. I thought of the other journals tucked neatly away on my bookshelves, whose pages held the history of my life's story, and vowed to go through them all, one by one.

Tomorrow I fly to New York, better prepared to stand in front of an audience than I have ever been.

REFLECTIONS

Journal entry

We are what we honor most.
We focus, we honor, we create.
Nothing more, nothing less.
We are what we see in ourselves.
We are alive to discover pure self,

Then to forget self and serve others.
We cannot teach what we do not know.

JIM BRITT

We cannot lead unless we know the way.
These are things I have learned

My greatest discoveries, however, have been made through simple things like cookies, angels and a child's love. And here I pen my deepest thoughts.

To love a child is to feel the warmth of Heaven.
When you take his hand, you venture to the stars.
When you see his dream and walk the path together,
You walk hand in hand with love in your heart.

One day he put his hand in mine and said, "come walk with me.
We'll walk the path together from the mountain to the sea.
We'll watch the pretty butterfly as it spreads its tiny wings.
And we'll sit and listen to the songs the bluebirds sing."

I took his hand, and together we walked among the flowers,
We watched the butterflies and ate cookies by the hour,
and softly whispered to the angels in the tree.
And through my child's eyes, I saw me.

Sometimes we walk in sunshine, sometimes the seas are tossed.
Then he holds my hand a little tighter, "Don't let go," he says, "or I'll get lost."
And as we travel through the dark and thunder, I begin to see,
At times I lead my little child, at times, he leads me.

Our lives are about special moments we experience. We don't remember all of our past but there are some things I will never forget.

The tenderness of a child's love,
The touch of his hand,
His kiss on my cheek,
His tears on my shoulder.

The tenderness of his heart,
The magic of his smile,
The wisdom in his eyes.
The beauty of his face.
These are the things I treasure

Thought for Today

We can't pursue and "catch" happiness,
it can't be possessed. Happiness is simply
a bi-product of letting go of what makes
you unhappy.

Chapter Three

Several years ago I would have found sitting in an airport inconvenient, boring and irritating. Today, I find it stimulating, interesting and even refreshing. My flight had been delayed because the weather in New York was in more turmoil than the weather here, so I decided to find a seat and enjoy the moment, which was not an easy task. The terminal was filled with people, some waiting for their plane to arrive, others, like me, waiting to board once it landed.

As I searched for a seat, my natural curiosity was aroused and I found myself more interested in the people around me than in finding the seat. There is a lot to be learned from people, all in the same situation, viewing it from different perceptions. Some, unlike me, had already found a seat and had come prepared with a book. Men and women groomed for the business world had briefcases open, while several teenagers, groomed for leisure, were lying on the floor, their heads propped up on their flight bags, sound sleep. I was reminded of the story about the ant and the grasshopper. The ant is busy all day gathering food for the winter while the grasshopper lounges in the shade, playing his fiddle. When winter comes, the ant, who had the foresight to think ahead, is secure in his ant bed with plenty of food to eat while the grasshopper is starving and shivering in the snow.

An updated version gives the story a different slant. The grasshopper isn't really lying around doing nothing but he is becoming a better fiddler. And, while his brain is at work devising new ideas, he makes friends with a butterfly who teaches him to fly. So, when winter comes, he had perfected his art of flying and flies south. He is now basking in the sun making beautiful music while the ant is shivering in his bed, under the snow, as he eats his crumbs.

I would introduce another version. While the ant is busy gathering the food for the winter, the grasshopper does his part by providing the music and song, because the world needs both ants and grasshoppers to survive. It takes both the serious and the artistic mind to create balance. While the ants in the airport are busy studying reports or clicking away at their computers, the grasshoppers just might be dreaming their way through a new symphony yet to be composed or a book yet to be written. I rather like this version.

Everywhere around me there were cell phones attached to ears, the buzz of conversation filtering the air. It seemed odd, in a way. A room full of people engulfed in conversation and yet the conversation wasn't in the room but in another space far removed. It had a ring of science-fiction to it. I smiled to myself as I envisioned the ant and the grasshopper in outer space

Sitting cross legged on the floor, leaning against the wall, sat a young man sketching from a book. His gray sweatshirt bore a university emblem and his levis had the fashionable tears across the knees. Even though his long dark hair concealed much of his face, the intention was still visible. I made my way to his side and without distracting him I watched as he captured on paper, faces full of emotion. His ability was extraordinary and I was captivated by his insight. He shadowed in the worried brow of a man pacing in front of him. He darkened, with heavy strokes, the anger showing in the face of a woman and highlighted the excitement in the smile on the face of a child. His hand was quick as he stroked the pencil but his eye was quicker as he uncovered the mask and reached into the soul.

For several minutes I stood there, unable to take my eyes off his work.

I wondered, did he have to reach inside himself to feel the emotion in order to interpret it on paper or could he remain abstract?

As if he had read my thoughts he looked up at me, smiled and said, "You have to almost sense the emotion of the face before you can sketch it. First, you feel it, then you sketch it. After that you just let it go. The fun part is that you can do it all without becoming involved with the emotion itself."

"I like your explanation," I replied as I slid down beside him, "but I thought artists were very emotional people."

He laughed as he started to sketch a likeness of me. "Depends on the depth of the artist, I suppose. I find sketching is a good way to release emotions as well as to understand them."

I was amazed at the speed in which he penciled my features. His trained eye catching in a glance all he needed to know. When he finished, he handed me an incredible likeness of myself on paper.

"You are a pretty tranquil guy who has mastered the aura of the airport, it makes you easy to sketch." He said. Before we could talk anymore, his flight was called so he closed his book, gathered his belongings and as he turned to leave he shook my hand and thanked me for the interest in his work. I thanked him for the sketch and watched him as he made his way through the crowd, having the feeling that he knew me almost as well as I knew myself. To an artist, faces are mirrors of emotion. I made a mental note to pay closer attention to faces.

I had failed to get the young man's name before he faded into the crowd but I will always remember his work and the wisdom of his words. I glanced again at the sketch to see if he had signed it. In the bottom right-hand corner were the initials C.T.

"Well, C.T." I said silently, "I hope to see your initials again someday."

The crowd was thinning out as flights were being called and I found a seat near the floor to ceiling window that framed a sky of dark clouds. The only evidence of the sun was a sprinkling of its rays above the darkness dramatizing the scene with the illusion of a halo. The silent rhythm of the rain as it touched the window was soothing and I wondered how many people sitting here, were listening.

I watched as a huge Boeing 747 taxied onto the runway in preparation for take-off. It's gigantic body vibrating with the power of the engines that would lift it into the air. It sat there, still for a moment, then began to move, gathering speed quickly until it severed its connection to the earth, and then, as if in slow motion, gracefully filled the sky with its presence.

As I watched the 747 disappear I wondered could Orville Wright have envisioned this incredible sight in his dream. Here is evidence of one man's vision and belief that he could fly. No, not simple belief but an infinite knowing from within.

But then, isn't that how great things happen? We first discover our idea through a dream . Then comes an understanding that allows the dream to evolve into a vision, then, from a vision to a goal which leads to action, which, in turn, produces the reality of the dream. Oftentimes there may be many realities produced in the process of refining one's original idea or dream.

Shakespeare penned the words, *"We know who we are but know not what we might be."* Is it the dream we dream, or an idea we conceive that takes us along that path to the person we can become? Of course it is. That is where we find our true self. Not at the end of the path, but along the way.

In a way, we are like planes. We are filled with equipment that controls us and determines whether we will sour gracefully into the sky or fail to even leave the ground. It all depends on how we operate that equipment. It depends on our vision. So often a person has a great, inspiring vision of something they want to create in life, then, just before lift-off, their limiting beliefs sabotage them and they never make it off the ground.

Our brain is like a computer filled with little chips, called dendrites, where thousands of bits of information are stored. Information filled with memories, experiences, feelings and beliefs. Everything we have learned, everything we are now learning will be stored on these chips as programs by which we live our lives. Every time we are put into a situation to re-experience or to open the original program through our thoughts, feelings, emotions or actions, whether positive or negative, we strengthen the original program. This is why it becomes so vitally important to let go of those programs that no longer support our life's vision. Otherwise when we decide to do a certain thing we rely on those old programs, good or not so much, to direct us.

We are continually creating the story of our lives, clicking and storing, clicking and storing, and strengthening each time we click and store, never stopping, day and night. It's as if we are wrapped in an invisible computer keyboard accessible to anyone around us. They can just type in their message and press enter, leaving us with a program that may or may not be constructive. Self-observation is critical here. We need to be aware of what's going on in our lives and the input we receive from others and our surroundings. We need to pay close attention to strengthening our productive programs and deleting the non-productive ones. What you pay attention to grow in strength. What you let go of withers away from lack of attention.

Once we are programmed, we continue to go forward, whether in leaps and bounds or by inches, or we go backward, or remain immobile, caught in an endless cycle, going nowhere, honoring our old beliefs. A human being is just like a flower, a tree or any other living thing. We continue to grow or die, physically, emotionally and spiritually in one way or another, it's all up to us.

The fuel that feeds our engines are the beliefs we carry, stored safely on board for use when needed. The problem is that all beliefs are false until we decide they are true. Even then it doesn't make them true.

We may all start as small single-engines but some grow into huge Boeing 747's while others stay, forever, single-engines.

As I was enjoying the moment, two women who appeared to be in their late sixties sat down to the right of me. Their dress told me they were wealthy. Nothing was out-of-place from their professional hairstyles to their expensive shoes. I almost felt casual in my tie and jacket. I could tell by the tone of their conversation they hadn't heard the soothing rhythm of the raindrops.

Glancing in the direction one woman's jeweled finger was pointing, I saw a group of young people dressed in very colorful and interesting apparel.

"It offends me," she said, " when I see young people wear clothing that suggests such disrespect to society. What can they be thinking as they parade around in next to nothing?"

"I certainly agree," the woman sitting next to her sighed in exasperation. "Why do they have to cut holes everywhere there is enough clothing to cover their bodies."

The two sat there for several minutes observing the happy group who was completely oblivious to the distress they were causing.

"Just look at their hair," the first woman continued, "every color of the rainbow."

A small elderly woman in her 80's leaned over to them, laughter in her eyes and commented. "Yes, and that's just on one head."

The two women looked at her with scorn for having invaded their privacy and turned away continuing their conversation in hushed tones.

As I watched the group and listened to the two women I thought to myself, we judge by our own standard of thinking. Like the two women, we may look at a person who isn't dressed to our standards and we say, *isn't it awful the way that person is dressed.* Or we could say, *isn't it interesting how they are enjoying life, differently than I do.*

Is it true, then, that they are dressed inappropriately? Evidently not in their way of thinking. Only to those who think so. Who would these two women be without this story?

They would be themselves allowing the young people to walk on by and have their own fun without judging them or taking on their issue. Would they be happier right now? I thought so.

And what about the happy group? Well, they have walked on by and are probably getting ready to board a plane for Hawaii or some exotic island, full of energy, completely unaware that they had interrupted the lives of two women.

A quiet voice spoke from the chair on my left. "You know those two seem to worry a lot about what is going on around them instead of just enjoying the view don't they?"

I turned and there she sat, the small elderly lady with the laughing eyes. Her soft white hair swirled around her face in a modern cut. Her small delicate hands folded properly on her lap, her lips pursed and her head tilted toward me, mocking the two she was speaking about.

I caught the gleam in her eye and I smiled back at her. "They seem to be using up a lot of energy taking on an issue in which they have no control." I replied.

She laughed and we introduced ourselves. She was waiting for her granddaughter to arrive on the same plane I would be flying out on so we had some time to visit.

"That little scene reminds me of a personal experience I had." she commented. "May I tell you the story? It's about a young man I met."

With interest, I gave her my full attention.

"He was about nineteen years old and very shabbily dressed," she began. "His hair was all matted and dirty. He came up to me and asked for a dollar. I just stopped and looked him in the face and said, young man you have so much potential. You have such beautiful blue eyes. If you washed your hair, I'll bet it would be a very pleasing shade of blond."

I saw strength in the face of this tiny woman and I was intrigued. I leaned a little closer. I didn't want to miss a word of her story.

"I have to tell you, it was something he did not expect to hear, especially from an old woman, but I just put my arms around him and gave him a hug. It's not the dollar, I told him, it's the potential that you have and I want to help you, but I'm not going to give you the dollar to help you.

I think because I believed in him he wanted to change. He got off the street and changed his life almost immediately and went on to do something with it, all because I cared enough not to give him a dollar but to see his potential. You know, we actually became the best of friends.

As I watched those young people walking by, instead of seeing ill dressed, disrespectable teens, I see potential. I see creativity. I hope they see it too someday," she concluded.

We sat there for ten more minutes talking before the plane from New York landed. We said goodbye, then she took my hand in hers and said. "How you live is a message to the world, go out and make someone's day." With those words she was off to greet her granddaughter.

Had my plane been on time I would have missed meeting two people of great worth to me, who each in their own way had touched my life and given it more meaning.

I boarded the plane for New York, found my seat, stored my travel bag and strapped myself in. Once all the preliminaries were taken care of and the plane was in the air, I leaned my head back and began to review in my mind the material for tomorrow's seminar.

I find when I am in a plane high above all that exists on earth, my mind clears. It's a phenomena I can't explain. My mind just opens up to ideas. Perhaps it's the humming sound of the engines that lulls me into a meditative state. I don't know, but I

have five hours to meditate on ideas I might add before the seminar begins at 9:00 tomorrow morning.

As I slipped my papers out of the brief case to finalize my plan for the seminar the woman sitting next to me asked, "It looks like you are flying to New York on a business trip. Would I be right?"

I smiled and introduced myself, explained quickly what I did and that I was on my way to New York to present a seminar on "Letting Go."

"That is interesting," she hesitated before going on. "You really help people let go of stuff?"

"Yes," I answered, "I guess you would say I'm a catalyst. I share ideas and ask questions. The people take the ideas, and what they learn about themselves as they answer my questions, and learn to let go."

She looked at me as if she was trying to decide whether or not to believe me. But, after a few moments of silence she leaned a little closer and spoke softly, "I have an issue I'm dealing with. Can you help me?"

We still had over four hours to New York so I consented. " What is it you are dealing with?" I asked.

"It's my husband," she replied. "We have been married for twenty years and he still doesn't know what marriage is all about."

For the next forty minutes she recited example after example of why her husband was the problem in their marriage. Finally, she stopped, turned and looked me in the eye. "So, can you help me?" she asked.

I thought for a moment as to how I should answer her and decided the direct approach would be the best. "Yes, but you won't like my answer," I explained.

"Why not?"

"Trust me, you won't like my answer." I said as definite as I could.

She argued, "Try me, just try me. I'm open."

I took a long breath. "Your husband is not the problem, you are." I said as gently as I could.

She looked at me as if I had touched her with an electric shock and her back turned to me so fast it almost took the plane off course. She didn't like my answer.

After about thirty minutes she hesitantly turned back toward me. Her mouth softened only slightly but she remained silent so I resumed. "You can't control what your husband does or doesn't do but you certainly can control your response. You're trying to control him. You're trying to make him something he's not, or do something he doesn't want to do. That is your problem. Maybe he is doing stuff you don't want in your life, but that's not the issue. The issue is what are you hanging on to."

She looked at me once again with angry eyes and turned her back. She didn't say another thing to me for two hours. She would not even look around when the flight attendant came by to ask if we wanted anything to drink.

I didn't disturb her. I thought it best if she had time to think about it. Maybe she would not speak to me again before the flight was over, or maybe she would. Either way I had given her something to think about.

Into her third hour of silence she turned and with sadness in her voice she admitted, "You are right. I have thought it through and I realize that now. I can't control him. All the pain I am going through has been brought on by me. Even though I would

like to have him be different, I can't make that happen. He has to decide that for himself."

She paused to gain composure, then continued, "But I still don't know what to do. Can you give me an example to follow?"

"Share one thing that your husband does that irritates you," I said.

Her response was immediate, "One thing that really irritates me is that he doesn't listen to me."

I asked, "How do you respond to him when you think he is not listening to you?"

"I get angry."

"How does he respond to your anger?"

"He shuts down." she said, and I sensed a touch of bitterness in her voice.

"And then what?" I asked

She looked me straight in the eye. "It makes me even more angry," she replied.

"The next question," I said, "I want you to think about before answering. The question is this; "is it true that he doesn't listen to you?"

Her eyes narrowed as she looked into my face. "Of course it is true that he doesn't listen to me."

I had a feeling she wanted to ask me if I was listening but before she could go on I asked, "How do you know it to be true?"

"Because," she replied, "he doesn't listen to me, that's how I know it to be true."

"Do you know, beyond a shadow of a doubt, that he's not listening to you?

Her mouth opened to respond, then she slowly closed it without saying a word and I could see she was really thinking about the question. After a moment her eyes met mine once again and she said, "I suppose there is no way I could really know for sure, unless I was him."

"So, it may not be true that he doesn't listen to you," I said.

Shaking her head, she answered, "I guess you are right. I hadn't looked at it in that way before."

My next question to you is; which comes first your anger or his shutting down? Do you get angry just thinking about talking to him?

Again looking at me in the eye; "I get angry just thinking about talking to him."

So, I asked, do you think that your anger may be triggering his shutting down?

"Wow! I never looked at it that way. So he is feeling my anger before I even start talking and shuts down before I ever open my mouth? Oh my God! I can see where I could be the problem."

My next question to you is; who would you be without your story?

"What story?" she asked quizzically.

"Your story that he doesn't listen to you."

"Well, I suppose I would be just me, without the anger." Again her thoughts were revealed in her face as she hesitated before continuing. "Yes, I would just be me without the anger."

"My next question is this; can you see any reason that isn't stressful or painful to hang onto your story?"

"No, I can't," she said simply.

"Stop for a moment and close your eyes and get in touch with the feeling you have when your husband doesn't listen to you." I waited about thirty seconds before continuing, "Do you feel it?"

"Yes, I do feel it."

"Do you like feeling that way?"

"No," she replied, "of course not."

"Do you want to let it go?"

"Yes, I do," was the answer.

"Are you willing to let it go and just be you?"

She hesitated for a moment so I asked again, "Are you willing to let it go and just be you?"

Finally, she was able to commit to an answer. "Yes, I am willing to let it go.

"My last question," I said, seeing the anticipation in her face, "When are you willing to let go of the need to control your husband?"

"Now," she answered without hesitation.

I asked her to take a moment and focus on the feeling once again. As she did she was amazed that the feeling was so light.

"Just focus on what you feel right now," I said, "and then breathe deeply and when you exhale, let it go."

I watched her face relax as she exhaled and I said once again, "Get in touch with the feeling once more."

She sat for a moment or two in silence. As tears of joy rolled down her face, she opened her eyes and said, "All I feel is me, no anger, just me. As much as I search, I cannot feel the anger toward my husband."

She patted my hand and thanked me for what I had done for her. We chatted for a few minutes longer while the plane landed and I explained that in a relationship you can either live with it as it is, negotiate a change or get out. In order for a relationship to remain healthy, you have to go into the relationship knowing what you are bringing into it. As soon as you bring love without expecting love in return then chances are, that is what you will receive in return. Then I handed her my card and asked. "Will you please let me know how your life is going?"

She seemed somewhat surprised that I would care that much and with a grateful smile she promised she would. We waved goodbye as we entered the terminal.

By the time I got to the hotel it was late. The urge to study my notes for tomorrow didn't hit me so I called home to let Joanna know I had arrived safely. Walker answered the phone instead.

"Hi ya' Dad," his little boy voice sounded excited through the receiver. "How was the plane ride?" Before I could say anything he continued, "Mom said, you'll be home on Friday, that's two days. I hope they go by fast because I've got some important stuff to discuss with you. Miss ya' Dad. Bye."

He hung up the phone. I sure hope he tells his Mother that I called.

I set my mental alarm clock and crawled into bed. I fell asleep wondering what important stuff Walker and I would be discussing on Friday afternoon.

Morning came and brought with it the early light of the sun giving me plenty of time to order a light breakfast. After fruit, muffins and juice, I showered and dressed and put on a jacket. At the last minute I decided to wear a tie.

I arrived at the seminar feeling very good about what I had to share with the audience. Nathan, who had coordinated the day, greeted me at the door and we discussed the make-up of the audience I would be addressing.

"Most of the people attending the seminar today," Nathan said, "are people who have heard about you through friends or brochures. There are some businesspeople who have the desire to be more successful in their businesses, but mostly you have people who want a change in their personal lives or in the lives of someone they care about. Some of them," he continued, "you may find, to be a little skeptical." Some are here because they have real concerns in their lives and are hoping for a miracle. Some came just to listen and learn. All in all, it should be a very rewarding day for all of you."

As everyone was getting seated I paid close attention to their faces pretending I was sketching them, and I was surprised by the revelation of emotion I received. I was attentive to the way they were dressed. It seemed to help me get a feel for the mood of the audience.

Most of the men had sport jackets on, maybe half of them wearing ties. The women were wearing either dresses or dress slacks. I was glad I had decided to put on the tie. I have always liked to dress for the occasion. Sometimes that means wearing jeans and a sport shirt and sometimes wearing a coat and tie.

Many years ago, I learned a lesson in dressing for the occasion, twice in one week. I was presenting a program for yacht brokers in Newport Beach, California. I wore a three-piece suit and they wore shorts and sneakers. A few days later, I was addressing a small group of bankers in Phoenix, Arizona. It was the middle of summer and very hot so I thought to myself, it's hot, everyone will be dressed casual, so I wore a casual shirt. They wore blue or gray suits and ties.

I made a decision, then, to always second-guess my audience and dress for the occasion. I'm firmly convinced the image one puts forth in business is important.

As the people waited, some talked, and some sat quietly, while others moved about shaking hands with strangers and introducing themselves. Some faces revealed pleasant smiles, while others shadowed their feelings behind lowered eyelids. There was an electrical feeling of anticipation in the room and I allowed its currents to charge me.

Nathan called the group to order and took some time talking about my books, *Rings of Truth*, and *Unleashing Your Authentic Power*, then gave me a generous introduction. I received a warm but conservative welcome applause from the audience.

I commenced with the usual opening of my presentation and then explained, "Life is a process and we each carry our own truths and our own beliefs which we'll talk more about later, but what I want you to do throughout this day is to have an open mind. There are some things you may not agree with because that may not be your truth or belief."

I had a woman call me after she had read *Rings of Truth*, and tell me there was one page that shouldn't be in the book.

I said simply, "Wow, ok."

She continued, "What do you have to say for yourself?"

There was really nothing I had to say for myself so I answered, "Nothing."

"Well, I don't think you should have put it there." Her words were sharp.

"Let me give you a suggestion, I replied, "If you have a magic marker handy just take it and X out that page or tear the page out completely."

"I don't want to tear up my book," she said. "I simply think you should have left it out."

"That's ok, that is your belief and your opinion. It's ok." I reassured her.

As I finished the story the audience chuckled, and I could sense an air of acceptance flow through the room. I let a brief moment pass while the mood was shifting in my favor then I continued.

"Maybe, like that woman, you aren't going to agree with everything but don't let it close your mind to the rest of what you will hear. There may be one little idea that you will take with you when you leave that will change your life forever."

Several heads nodded in agreement as I continued. "First, I want to share with you my theory of energy and the universe. We arrive here on earth with a certain amount of energy to use up. Let's call it 'cosmic' energy or whatever. We can burn up our allotment of energy however we choose. We are human beings. We have free will. We can create. We have imaginations and we can use that energy for whatever purpose we choose. But as soon as we burn all of it up, our trip gets canceled."

Demonstrating in the air I explained, "Here is a galaxy inside the universe. How big is a galaxy? It might be two hundred and fifty thousand light years across. Then, there is another galaxy and another until we see Earth. So from the first galaxy to Earth, let's say, is one million light years. Consider, you would travel at the speed of light, one hundred and eighty-six miles a second for a million years to get across, five galaxies. Here we are on earth, in the middle of this galaxy. Now when you take a look at the whole, how many galaxies are there in the universe?"

"Unlimited," was the response offered by the audience.

"In relation to the whole," I asked, "how big is our galaxy?"

It was decided that even though it was 250,000 light years across, it was actually pretty small when you take into consideration the entire universe.

"So, our galaxy seems pretty small among the millions of galaxies, doesn't it? Now, imagine earth and put it into the center of our galaxy. It would seem pretty small compared to that galaxy because it is only a few thousand miles in circumference. It's two hundred and fifty thousand light years across the galaxy and you could travel around the earth in about a twenty-four hour period. Got the picture?" I asked. I wanted them to get the idea of how small we really are in comparison to the whole.

"Now, let's go a step farther. If you take earth and compare it to the universe, how small does it seem?"

It was a unanimous decision among the audience that the earth was pretty small in comparison.

"Now, if you think of you on the earth and compare you to the universe, how big are you? Not even a speck. Now if you take your problems and compare them to the universe, how big are they? They are pretty simple. We only make them universal."

There were broad smiles and short chuckles throughout the audience as the picture was painted in their minds of how microscopic they and their problems would appear in the vastness of the universe.

"You really are the center of the universe and here you are burning up your allotment of energy. You can burn it up however you wish. You can burn it up as fast or as slow as you want, because we have been given free will, choice and imagination to do so."

I then told them the story of the two women in the airport, and how they were burning up energy over something so trivial as the preferred dress of several young people.

"Here's the question," I continued, "how much of their allotted energy did they burn during the ten minutes they chose to be critical of a scene over which they had no control? How much time of their trip on earth did they use? Maybe minutes. Or hours. Maybe a day or perhaps even as much as a whole month."

The sound of the morning traffic could be heard and it reminded me of an experience I had to share.

"Ever get stuck in traffic" I smiled, "and running late for an important appointment? I'm sure we all have. Let's say that you were traveling down the freeway at seventy miles per hour and you have about five miles to go. You figure if you continue at this speed, you'll be at your appointment on time. All of a sudden some idiot, pulls in front of you and slows the traffic down to sixty-five. Right away you begin to get upset, burning up energy. You have no time to waste, you've got to be on time. You finally see a ray of hope, your exit. What happens? Right! He pulls off in front of you on the exit.

The road splits into a right and left lane and you are going right. You're saying to this idiot, "go left, go left!" He goes right. You now see the driveway into the parking lot. What does he do?"

The audience was one step ahead of me. They were pursing their lips and nodding their heads up and down.

"You've been behind him too, have you?" I laughed. "Late model, expensive car, white with a convertible top, right?"

One gentleman commented with a loud chuckle. "He drove the blue Buick the day he pulled out in front of me."

I nodded, "And when you pulled into the parking lot, he pulled right in, in front of you, correct?"

After the chuckles died down I continued with the story. "You finally get out of your car and you are furious at this idiot for all the time he has cost you and you're going to give him a piece of your mind...what little you have left. You walk up to his window and begin to shout, 'Do you know how much time you have cost me?' You look at your watch and quickly calculate. 'You have cost me thirty seconds.'

Here's the real question you should be asking. How much time have you cost you? How much of your energy allotment have you just burned up trying to control something over which you have no control? That's the important question. You just never know when your allotment is going to run out."

The audience responded once again to the picture I had painted in their minds. To most of them the story hit home and they nodded their heads in the affirmative.

"Let's say," I continued, "that you are going to the bathroom. You are in there doing your thing when, suddenly, you realize there is no toilet tissue. You are furious! Out loud you say to yourself, 'How many times have I told those kids...'" Bam!! Your trip gets canceled. It's over for you and that's where they find you, sitting on the toilet, and that's ok, you have free will."

Laughter filled the room, then it died down and silence took its place once again. "You can choose to burn up your allotment any way you choose. There is no right or wrong way, whatever way you choose is alright."

As I looked around the room, I could see by the face of each person in the audience, they were in deep reflection, remembering all the foolish ways they had chosen to burn their allotment.

I paused for a moment allowing them this time of reflection then I continued. "There's a word I believe to be the most important word in the English language, resourcefulness. When you define it at its root meaning, it means, *once again full of source*.

"Source" is defined in Webster's Dictionary as, where all things originate. In ancient text source is defined as *Love*. Re-source-ful - "*once again full of love.*" If all things originate in source and source is love then all things originate in love, and love is energy. It's the energy we use when we stimulate our imaginations or exercise our free will."

Several people in the audience were writing down the definitions as I spoke so I stopped for a moment while they finished before continuing.

"So, either we are being resourceful or we are not. Either we are full of love, of source, or we are not. Either we have let go, or we have not. It's that simple.

The question should always be: Is the thought I'm thinking, the action I'm taking, the belief I'm holding, the emotion I'm experiencing, resourceful or non-resourceful? Is

it based on love? Is it moving me closer to what I would love to have in my life or further away. Life is really that simple.

To be alive is to have problems and that's why we are here in the first place, to figure out our problems and to discover our true selves through our solutions. In fact, if you are alive and you don't have problems, then you've got real problems!

Someone told me the other day, 'You know very few people have common sense,' to which I replied, 'No, everyone has common sense. Very few people have uncommon sense.'

That's what we are going to work on today, uncommon sense. I call it correct thinking instead of just glossing over an issue with positive thinking. We are going to get things down to being simple where we can understand them.

Let's say, for example, that you want a loving relationship and you are in an argument. Who wins in an argument?"

An elderly gentleman on the second row raised his hand and answered boldly, "No one and I should know I have had plenty of experience, young man, believe me. And if no one wins that means both parties involved loses, and that's a fact."

The audience responded with laugher and I could see the atmosphere relaxing even more.

"Thank you sir, you've just made my point," I continued. "Are we being resourceful or non-resourceful in that case? Are we going to resolve an issue by arguing about it? People who argue just want to be right, don't they? I don't care if it hurts me and you, I just want to be right.

We have to let go of our need to be in control and decide what is best for both parties involved. But the first person you want it to be best for is you. See life is not about the other person. It's about you. A relationship is not about the other person. Your job is not about your boss, your relationship with your kids, or your spouse. It's not about them. It's about you.

Ask yourself what you really want in life and then ask yourself, WHY? Keep asking yourself *why* until you get to the pure essence. When you get to the essence of what you want then ask yourself, "How would that make me feel? What would I be doing different in my life?"

Once you get to the real reason, find the feeling behind it then you can live in a dream fulfilled. Only by knowing what you want and how it would make you feel to have that, can you truly know if you are bring resourceful or non-resourceful. If you don't know what you really want, how would you know if an action you are taking is going to move you in that direction? In other words, decide what you want, then start feeling that way now. Another way of saying it is, to decide what you want and then love it into your life.

If you want peace of mind, you have to let go of the anxiety. Peace of mind isn't served to you on a silver platter, it comes to you in the form of anxiety. I suppose it's love's way of saying, 'If you want more of me, you have to handle this.' It's easy to stay the way we are but we have to ask ourselves, is that being resourceful or non-resourceful? And how do we know if we don't know what we really want in our lives.

Each one of our experiences in life creates our beliefs or what we see as truths. Our truths become our story. Think of an experience in your past that was painful. Anything, a hurt, a failure, something someone did to you, something you did to someone else...anything. Think of the feeling it created. When did it start? Recall when it ended, if it has? I want you to share with me the number of years, months or days."

There was an emotional silence in the room and a stillness in the audience that lasted for a short period of time, then, as if a calendar had been set in place, one gentleman hesitantly said, "four years,"

"Fourteen years," A young woman on the front row whispered.

"Ten years, twelve years, twenty-two years," others called out.

Then one woman, four rows back, responded. "Forty-five years," she exclaimed.

It sounded like I was auctioning something off to the highest bidder. Just to break the tension that was building, I said, "Sold to the woman with forty-five years."

Smiles crossed the faces of the audience and I continued. "Now, I would like you to ask yourself if hanging onto that feeling is resourceful or non-resourceful? Does hanging onto it bring you more happiness, peace of mind, success? Is it based on love?"

Once again a silence settled over the room as memories began to surface in the minds and hearts of those willing to let them flow. You could see it in their faces.

When the time felt right I asked if anyone would like to share their story. Everyone seemed to be waiting for someone else to speak. Finally, a woman on the third

row raised her hand. "I would like to share an experience," she said quietly, "if it will help me or anyone else in this room."

I invited her to share her story.

"My husband told me the other day that I wasn't his best friend," she spoke hesitantly.

"And how did that make you feel?" I asked

"Devastated," she remarked. "I had no idea."

"Do you know that to be true or did he just say it without thinking about what he was saying?" I asked.

"He meant it," she replied.

"Do you still feel devastated?"

"I don't know if I feel devastated now but it has brought me a feeling of great loneliness," she answered.

"Did the fact that he told you that you were no longer his best friend make you feel lonely?" I asked.

"No," she responded. "The loneliness comes from the fact that I am now alone."

It was important that she understood what I was trying to communicate to her so I proceeded more deliberately. "I want to ask you, how would you feel if you didn't experience loneliness? You would still be alone but how would you feel?"

She thought for a moment before answering. "More content, I suppose."

"Ok, can you see any reason to hang on to the loneliness that isn't painful or stressful?"

"No," she replied.

"So there is no reason to hang onto it. So do you want to feel content?"

She lifted her eyes and looked into mine with determination. "Yes, yes I do."

"Do you want to get rid of loneliness?" I asked.

She nodded.

The audience, as if they were one, nodded with her. They had, in a sense, become a part of her story. They wanted her to let go of the loneliness as much as she wanted to let go. The emotion in the room was tingling.

"The main thing," I continued, "is to look at the loneliness and get to the truth behind it. It is true that your husband said, 'You are not my best friend anymore.' But is it true that is the cause of your loneliness?"

"No," she admitted.

"Who would you be without the loneliness?"

"I would just be me," she replied.

"Can you think of one good reason you should hang onto something that would cause you pain or stress?" I asked.

"No," she answered.

"Ask yourself, ' Do I want this in my life?' "

The woman looked at me as if she was trying to fully comprehend what I was suggesting.

"But how do I get rid of it?" she asked.

"Do you want this in your life?"

"No."

"Who is the most important person in the relationship?"

She hesitated before asking, "Me?"

"You sound as if you're not sure." I said, then I posed the same question, but in another way. "Who's happiness is most important, yours or your husband's?"

"My happiness is most important. I hadn't thought of it that way before, but it has to be mine." She was reaching inside and her feelings were beginning to surface. "I am the most important person in the relationship. My happiness is the most important." As tears rolled down her face, she spoke with a strength she was feeling for the first time.

"Do you want to become a loving person again?" I asked.

"Yes," she answered with enthusiasm.

"Without the loneliness you can do just that. Whatever we feel inside, we create more of in our lives. So if you are feeling lonely and you trap that as an experience there is not the capacity to have an open heart and have love in a relationship, or even self-love in a relationship with yourself. Once we become a loving person we attract loving relationships."

I asked the same question once again. "Do you want to become a loving person again?"

"Yes," she cried with full commitment. "Yes, I do."

"Then just take a deep breath and let go of the loneliness," I said gently.

Silence followed as everyone in the room anticipated her breath, and the emotion was stimulating and warm as they joined in her experience of letting go.

As the day progressed more people shared experiences with the group and a feeling of unity engulfed us. Some of the men had taken off their jackets. Some had even loosened their ties.

I explained that when people have the courage to be self-observant, they can see whether they are holding onto something that is getting in the way of their resourcefulness. Resourcefulness is our natural state, full of source, full of love, full of happiness. It is in this natural state we are able to experience the moment, and where we are able to experience self-love. By letting go of our ego-driven needs, we are able to return to who we truly are; resourceful, loving, happy, creative beings. All we need to do is to observe, let go, become resourceful, and then take action. Without it we cannot grow. Without it we cannot develop the gifts that we have been given in this life.

Resourcefulness is the ultimate state of *response-ability* in which we respond with the most clarity to the events and circumstances that are presented to us.

When we allow someone else to write our story, we become the victim, the co-star, if you will, or the extra on the set, and we are taken out of our resourceful place. We have lost our identity because we are lost.

The same can happen when we attach ourselves to another person's story. We again are taken from our resourceful place. We have, in a sense, given our power to someone else.

"To find our true nature of happiness we have to begin by taking responsibility for writing our own story and for the players on the set," I emphasized, "for observing how you feel by letting go of those things that do not empower you to take resourceful action. Instead of saying,

'Why does this always happen to me?' Take the resourceful approach and say, 'What feeling am I hanging onto that attracts this painful situation?' Instead of saying, 'How do I relieve my anxiety?' Say, 'What feeling am I hanging onto that's causing me to feel anxious?' Instead of saying, 'Why is this person acting this way?' Say, 'Why should I suffer over how anyone else is acting?' Instead of asking, 'If God really exists, why doesn't he help me?' Try a more resourceful approach by asking, 'What can I do to help myself?' Instead of saying, 'Why is this person treating me this way?' Ask yourself, 'What feeling am I hanging onto that causes me to want to be the victim in someone else's story?' This is self-observation in action.

Observe yourself feeling sorry for yourself and ask, how come I have created such a stupid drama for myself and what do I need to do to make a change? Make up your mind, starting right now, that you will not settle for anything less than resourcefulness in your life. Write your story the way you want it to be.

Remember, what you see and experience is who you are and who you are is what you'll see and experience. It's the law of cause and effect in action. End of story!

Resourcefulness allows us to be open for the miracles to take place in our lives. Einstein once said, 'You can live your life as if everything is a miracle or as if nothing is a miracle.' Either one is ok.

Resourcefulness helps you to be open to solutions to your problems instead of being blinded by them. It helps you have open vision instead of tunnel vision. When we have tunnel vision we focus in on the problem and we are blinded by the problem itself. When we have open vision and are able to see the real truth behind our problems, we become solution oriented.

Helen Keller stated it perfectly when she said, "Worse than being blind is having eyes to see and having no vision."

At the end of the day I summarized by connecting resourcefulness and energy together with the statement, "How we utilize the energy in the resourceful state or burn up the energy in a non-resourceful state is completely in our control. We can only decide for ourselves which state we prefer. Either one is ok. It's just good to know that we have a choice.

If it requires letting go to achieve the state we desire, then let go. If not, then don't. It's as simple as that."

The day had gone very well. I had added the story of the young man who, because an elderly woman cared, took the responsibility to change his life. I told about the angels and "Mr. Britt's Cookies".

As I closed with a summary of the day, I looked into the faces and I saw smiles and nods of approval. The tone of the room had changed dramatically. I once again concentrated on the faces before me and I saw faces that were happier, faces that were lighter. Even some that looked younger. As I watched I decided that letting go can have a genuine effect on a person's body, mind, emotions and spirit. If they didn't agree with everything I had shared, at least I knew they were taking home an idea that had the potential to change their lives.

I finished to an enthusiastic round of applause and several handshakes and hugs of gratitude. People stopped at the table where the two previous books I had written and some audio albums were being displayed. Several bought books, others bought the audios and most of them picked up a brochure on the three day workshop that I schedule at least three times each year. I felt the day had been a success as I spent the next forty minutes signing books and answering questions.

As I unlocked the door to my hotel room I was feeling pretty good about life. Once inside I set the key on the table and, without turning on a light, walked to the window where a breathtaking view of the city awaited me. Buildings towered around me, lit up like Christmas trees. Thirty-four stories below, Time Square, dressed in all its finery, offered its brilliance to the setting. It was postcard perfect.

Taxi's, the size of matchbox cars, and people lining the sidewalk the size of ants, were moving in all directions giving the scene an appearance of animation.

I'm standing here by the window trying to describe the whole thing to myself when songs can't even catch, in their lyrics, the hypnotic beauty of New York City at night.

Giving up on the idea I pulled a comfortable looking overstuffed chair close to the window, sat down and just let myself feel the experience. It gave new meaning to the saying, *A picture is worth a thousand words.*

I began to feel the small of my back mold itself to the chair and I let my mind slip into nothingness. When I opened my eyes, the sun was lighting the room.

I arrived at the airport in plenty of time and feeling great. The trip home was uneventful and my car was waiting in the airport parking lot when I arrived. I threw my travel bag in the trunk, climbed in behind the steering wheel and let the car take me home.

I watched the pine trees come into view as I neared my destination. I never tire of seeing them expand from little seedlings to majestic overseers in just a few minutes. It's like observing Mother Nature at work at an accelerated speed. I don't think even the night lights of New York City can hold a candle to this. In trees you find reverent beauty, unsurpassed. I love trees.

As I turned onto the road that led to my driveway, I had a sudden urge to stop the car, turn off the key, pick up my note pad and take a walk. So, I did. I let my feet take me wherever they pleased, and within a few minutes found myself standing in front of a large flat rock. The perfect spot to sit and write my thoughts of the past two days while they are still fresh. I sat, still, for several minutes, watching the trees in the distance and letting the afternoon breeze cool the heat of the sun on the back of my neck before taking out my pen. Before I put anything on paper, however, I reminded myself to be sure and hug a tree when I got home.

REFLECTIONS

Journal entry

I am sitting here thinking that every time I return from a seminar, I return with more knowledge than when I left.

> *I watched as other lives echoed around me*
> *I listened to the silent rhythm of the rain*
> *I witnessed the artist's touch, a woman's wisdom,*
> *And I shall never be the same.*
>
> *A plane lifts off the ground because of one man's vision*
> *It spreads its wings and sours into the sky.*
> *It mattered not what others tried to tell him,*
> *Within his heart, he knew that man could fly.*
>
> *I am reminded of a thought by Shakespeare.*
> *"We know who we are but not what we can be."*
> *We, like planes, can sour, or have no lift off.*
> *We decide our fate, for we are free.*
>
> *In every human being there is a spotless beauty.*
> *And unlimited potential, only God can give.*
> *He hands us each our trials and then He tells us,*
> *"It's you that must decide which way you'll live."*

We are here and we are free to capture every problem
And discover our true self through solutions that we find
But, we must only search within to win the battle
For that is where we'll find our peace of mind.

If we were to search the universe, I wonder what answers we would find out there that could bring us to a full understanding of who we are. This I do know. In our search, we choose how to use the allotment of energy we have been graciously given by the universe.

We are the center
We are creative
We have imaginations
We have free will.

We are full of source, but we must know it
We are full of love, but we must feel it
On this earth, we create who we are.

Thought for Today

Create your vision of what you want in life,
Then play with whomever shows up to play.

Chapter Four

As I pulled up I could see Joanna's car was gone. A little disappointed I parked the car on the driveway, opened the door and inhaled the fresh air that surrounded me. It was good to be home.

I looked around for Walker. I was looking forward to discussing the important stuff with him but, instead, Weston greeted me.

"Hi Dad," he shouted from the backyard. "How did your seminar go yesterday?"

"It went well." I replied as I opened the trunk of the car to retrieve my travel bag. "Had about a hundred people there." I smiled as I heard his voice coming closer.

"Cool. Need some help?" he asked.

A sensational feeling of love swept over me as I reached out, grabbed him and gave him a bear hug. He hugged right back.

"Glad you're home," he laughed as he let go and reached for my weathered looking flight bag. "Might want to invest in a new one of these someday as much as you use it. So, what did you talk about in your seminar?"

I watched Weston as he threw the flight bag over his shoulder and I remembered a time in my life when I traveled with only the finest luggage, and even aspired to own a white limousine.

I remembered how Alea had used the desire for the limousine to bring me to a new level of understanding.

"*Why did you want the limousine?*" she had asked in her soft yet penetrating voice.

The answer was simple, "Because it would make me look successful."

"*Why do you want to look successful?*" She asked, and continued asking why with every answer I gave her. I found I had to reach deeper into my mind and into my heart to find the answers until, at last, I found the answer she was waiting to hear, and I realized the line of questioning had come to a full circle and I could answer truthfully, "I want more love and I want to be more loving."

She had smiled and stated simply, "*that is a far cry from the white limousine.*"

When Alea felt she had reached the pure essence of my soul and the depth of my learning, she asked, *what is love?*

The answer was clear. Love was standing before me holding a weathered flight bag over his shoulder. Love was Weston who twelve years ago brought with his birth an incredible capacity to love unconditionally. He literally cares about everyone, how they feel, what they think.

I realized the purity of his love when he was eight years old and we were driving down a street in San Francisco. We had all packed a lunch for a picnic in the park and

had stopped at a light when he pointed toward the side of the street and asked, "What is that person doing?"

I looked where his finger was pointing and saw a street person digging through the garbage.

Joanna tried to explain that he was probably looking for food.

"In the garbage?" Weston asked, his eyes showing the confusion he felt.

"He probably doesn't have any money to buy food and has to find it wherever he can," Joanna said, knowing her words sounded hollow.

"But not in a garbage can!" he cried. "Stop the car, please, Dad, and I will give him my lunch."

My heart started to swell as I quickly found a place to park close to where the man was standing. Weston got out of the car, walked up to him and handed him the lunch sack, then he got back into the car and said simply, "Ok, let's go."

That day, as I watched Weston walk away from the car, his shoulders square, his eyes lifted toward the stranger, I discovered my son was not afraid to give from his heart.

I became painfully aware that I had been going through life with my heart half closed and my son, through his example, was showing me how to open my heart and keep it open.

That day my teacher was an eight-year old boy who taught me to be who I am and to come from my heart. He helped me discover that when your heart is filled to capacity with unconditional love, you cannot close it. It has to remain open all the time. It is the only way you can be aware of those who might need part of that love.

That day my teacher was a homeless man who helped me understand that love is not a feeling of convenience but one of tremendous influence. I wonder if the experience made a difference in his life. Could he see through his pain what a little boy saw in him? Someone to love! I hoped he had.

Sometimes people go through life without realizing that the pain they are feeling is the pain of being closed to receiving love. We must be able to open our hearts to receive love before it can be open and ready to give love, for without receiving we have no capacity to give.

Thank you, Alea, my heart whispered, thank you for teaching me that love is the greatest gift we can receive and give. A gift so valuable that to lose it is to lose life. A flutter stirred my heart as the words, *you are welcome, Jim,* were felt more than heard.

I turned my attention back to the handsome young man carrying the once expensive flight bag and I smiled. What a contrast in value. A twelve-year old boy just beginning to shine and a ten-year old bag that had lost its luster long ago. A deep sense of gratitude for this young man who still carried within his heart the gift of love, flowed through me so swiftly I felt light-headed. Today his heart was open to me. He was genuinely interested in hearing about the seminar.

"Well," I explained as I closed the trunk, "I had planned on concentrating on letting go but resourcefulness got in the way."

"Ah, one of the most powerful words in the English language, right?" he was saying as he winked, and set the flight bag down by the trailer we are living in while our home is being built.

"Do you think resourcefulness would get our home built faster?" he smiled.

"Only if we intend to finish it ourselves," I reminded him.

Before us stood a magnificent unfinished structure that had seen several different stages of completion in the past thirteen months. Five months ago we said we were going to move into the house in three months. The lease was up on the house we were living in and it seemed foolish, at the time, to sign a new lease for three months, so we bought a travel trailer. There were only six of us and three months wasn't that long.

We had only one problem. We kept making changes in the building plans and one day the building inspector came to inspect.

"Let's see," he said as he went over the plans and walked through the house, "there's a door here on your plans and now you have a window. Over here, you have a door where they show a window. Mmmmm, this wall has been moved eight inches." Each time he would note a change from the blueprints, he would slowly nod his head and murmured a soft aa-hummm. After his inspection was complete, he rolled up the plans and in a matter-of-fact way stated, "We'll need to red-tag this structure until a whole new set of plan specifications, showing all the changes, has been drawn up. Not only that, but they will also have to be re-engineered with new energy calculations." Then he climbed in his truck and rode away.

Everything stopped for three months while we waited for new plans and we have lived in the travel trailer for six months instead of three with a few more months ahead of us.

Weston pulled two lawn chairs close together so we could sit and discuss the seminar. It was a beautiful warm day in Grass Valley. A day to sit and listen as the musical sounds of nature connecting with the rhythm of the breeze. The sun, inviting itself to the party, played hide and seek with the clouds bouncing shadows on the trailer behind us.

"You know," Weston spoke into the silence, "I suppose living in this trailer as long as we have could get rather boring after a while, but not here. I call this really livin'." Then he pointed toward the house that will someday be finished. "Look, can you see the deer? There are three more just like him that come every day. I saw two red foxes playing in our meadow, yesterday, and last week I saw a Golden Eagle flying overhead. I hope they never quit coming. This is such a great place to live, Dad."

"Well put," I replied, feeling my body relax. The past two days had been hectic and sitting here with Weston, watching the deer and experiencing the sensation of complete peace felt almost hypnotic.

The breeze filled the air with the smell of fresh pine as it flowed through the trees undisturbed and I said, "Before we go in, let's go take a walk around the property."

"Sounds good to me," Weston murmured back.

"I suppose living in the trailer for six months could get quite stressful if you let it." I sighed lazily.

"Or you can go day to day and enjoy wherever you are right now. If you're in a trailer, enjoy the trailer," he laughed as he patted the side of the trailer behind him.

I let my eyes wander to the trailer and then back to Weston. He was right, we could stay focused on the house that's not yet finished and be upset because it's taking so long and we have to live in a small trailer, or, we could just be happy living in the trailer while watching our home being built. In other words, we could be upset now and wait for our happiness, or we could just be happy with what we have.

"My words, exactly." I reached back and patted the trailer.

We walked watching the clouds as they bunched and puffed and spread themselves across the sky.

Weston pointed to a cloud to the right of us. "See that cloud?" he asked. "What does it remind you of?"

I watched the cloud for several seconds trying to recognize some form but finally had to admit. "Nothing in particular." I said, wondering what he could see. "Maybe potential to be a rabbit or a dog."

"Isn't that great, Dad?" he replied, "It doesn't have to worry about pleasing anyone, it can be whatever it wants to be because no one sees anything in particular in its form, only potential. Now watch as it floats, the atmosphere molds it and gives it direction," excitement filling his voice as he continued. "See what's happening?"

As the cloud moved the rays of the sun were caught in its billowing wisps and it began to change from nothing in particular to something beautiful beyond description. The cloud was still the cloud but it seemed to delight in the moment. The sun saw the cloud's potential, we, in turn, witnessed the transformation.

"It's kind of like this trailer," he said in a hushed tone. "It isn't anything in particular until we all step inside, then it becomes something beautiful because love has filled it with a radiance. So, don't feel too bad that we're still waiting after all this time. We are still the same people whether we are in the house or in the trailer. You just have to let go and enjoy this moment." He smiled in jest.

Weston was right. We could get caught up in the fact that we're still in the trailer, but no matter how upset we get we can't change what's happening and we won't get into the house any sooner.

It's not that I hadn't tried. I had gone to the county and told them, "You don't understand. This is where I am and I'm moving into this house."

They told me, in return, "You don't understand, you're not moving into it until it is finished." And we haven't.

"So, let's talk seminar, Dad." Weston said as we continued our walk around the property.

" Well, we talked about the fact that each one of us has a story we are living right now, right this minute." I looked at Weston and laughed. "Like our story we are living right now in our trailer, to the side of our home that is yet to be finished. This is our story. We could sit here stressed out over the fact that we are still living in a trailer after six months, but who would we be with all the stress? We'd be Weston and Dad still sitting here living in a trailer all upset. Who would we be without that story? We'd be Weston and Dad still sitting here living in a trailer talking and relaxing. Which is best? We have a choice, you and I. We choose to delete the stress from our story."

"Like a computer," Weston interjected, "We don't like how stress makes us feel so we push 'delete', and the stress is gone. He smiled at me, his eyes full of humor. "Want to finish telling me about your seminar on our way to the other end of the property?"

"Let's just walk and enjoy the moment." I grinned.

As we walked toward the big oak at the corner of the property, its beauty stood out. It was as if it had been painted there, it's limbs formed with perfection in mind. Joanna had taken a picture of it last week to take to her mother who is dying of cancer. It is under this tree that she intends to communicate with her mother after her mother leaves this world.

"I want my mother to see this picture so she will know where to meet me when I need to talk to her after she dies," Joanna had said, sadness filling her voice as she carefully placed it in an envelope.

As we walked past the house-in-progress, Weston motioned toward the back yard. "How much resourcefulness would you need to convince the rattle snakes back there to find a new home? Walker saw one this morning by the rock but I couldn't find it this afternoon."

"Where is Walker?" I asked. "I thought he would be here waiting. He has some important stuff to discuss with me."

"He's with Mom. They went to the library to find some books on rattlesnakes I think. You know Walker. He has decided if he can learn all about them, their habits and what they eat he will find a way to get them to go live somewhere else. Ok, so which tree do you want to hug. We have a choice of many."

"I'll take the old oak," I said. "You can have your choice of the others."

We laughed as we walked toward the trees. Hugging trees had become popular in the family several months ago when we found that hugging trees is good for the soul, in a matter of speaking. Nature is therapeutic because it is so relaxing. Take a tree, for example, they only live in the present, and when we get into the present we feel connected. That's when we feel a sense of love, for love only happens in the present. It does not exist in the past or the future, only now. It's because we live with certain fears taught by our past, or fear of what the future might hold, that we find ourselves out of the moment. That's why it's good to take time to hug a tree.

After we each hugged a tree we walked along one of the several paths the boys had made around the property.

"This reminds me of the story of 'Alice in Wonderland'," Weston said as he was deciding which path to take next.

"Alice in Wonderland?" I asked. "Why's that?"

"When Alice finds herself in Wonderland she doesn't know which way to go, the paths all lead in different directions. She meets the Cheshire Cat and she asks him, *Which way do I go from here?*

The cat says to her, *That depends on where you are going.*

Then Alice says, *I don't know where I'm going.*

To which the cat replies, *Then it doesn't matter which way you go.*

Do you remember that part?" he asked.

"I had forgotten that part but you brought it back to my memory," I answered, wondering where this was leading.

"I wonder, do we always have to know where we are going before we can get to where we really want to be, or can we find out where we really want to be by taking an unknown path?"

"That is rather a complicated question," I replied.

"Ok," he said, "what if you always took the path that was the straightest, or the smoothest. There were no rocks messing up the way or ugly vines hanging down, and you could see the horizon because there were no heavy dark forests to go through, it was all bricked and brushed. But, when you got to the end you weren't any happier than when you started, in spite of the smooth path, because you weren't where you really wanted to be?"

"Did you learn something along the way?" I asked.

"Yeh, you learned that you didn't want to be there."

"Why?"

"Because you didn't find what you wanted."

"What did you want?"

"You don't know until you get to the end of the path." He smiled. "Do you see what I mean, Dad?" he asked.

"On the other hand," I suggested, "what if you took the rocky path, with vines blocking the way and just when you get the vines cut down you see a dark forest ahead of you? You begin to wonder, how deep is the forest and what lies beyond it? What if there's a wide river to cross or cliffs to climb in order to continue on the path. Would it be worth a journey into the unknown, not having any knowledge as to whether or not what you are seeking is at the end? Would it be worth everything you have to go through to get to it?"

"Now you are getting the idea." Weston's eyes lit up as he spoke. "How do you decide what path to take or does it matter which one you take, because if it's not the right one you can just come back and choose another one."

"Or," I pointed out, "what if you knew that the path of least resistance would bring you a little bit of what you want and you could be a little bit happy but only the path with all the obstacles would take you to a place where you would find exactly what you were looking for, and would bring you true happiness. Which one would you take?"

"What if," his smile turned to a full grin, "you took several, on each one learning stuff that would help you discover what it was you really wanted. Then, you come back one more time to the beginning and take the right path because now you know. The only way to find the right one, however, is to travel many."

I looked at my son, "What you are saying," I said, "is that it is the discoveries you make along the way that help you decide those things that will make you happy and sometimes it is in choosing the wrong path and finding what happiness is not, that you find the right path and true happiness."

"Right," he put his arm around my shoulder as he spoke. "Isn't it true that some people always take the path they are familiar with and, therefore, never get to where they want to be, while others step into the unknown and find exactly what they want and they didn't know it until they had courage enough to take the step?"

"Maybe," I said, "while everyone is searching for the correct path to truth, the real truth is there is no correct path except the one we create for ourselves and the only way to find it is through self-observation because we have learned nothing if we learn nothing about ourselves in the journey."

"That's a good point," he commented. "If we are always looking down the road to tomorrow how can we experience today?"

"It seems," I continued, " that when we are in the midst of all our obstacles and the pain they create, all of our energy is focused on getting away from the pain, and not on what we might be able to learn from it. If, when the pain has lifted and we can reflect on our suffering and seek to develop an understanding of its meaning, we will find, within ourselves, a strength we hadn't known before. We must not forget, however, to also look for the meaning when things are going well."

"Have you ever thought, Dad, Weston said as he dropped his arm from my shoulder, and turned around to look at the oak tree, "how much human nature and mother nature operate from the same premise? I mean, look at that beautiful old oak tree. How strong would you say its roots are? Strong enough to withstand the most violent storm?"

"I would think so," I replied. "But the tree didn't grow its roots just as a storm appeared on the horizon. It had to develop them as it grew."

"Exactly! And, with each small storm it survived, it grew stronger until it could withstand even the most violent storm of them all." With that he motioned to me and we began to walk toward the trailer again.

The path of self-discovering, I thought to myself as we walk for a distance in silence, is enjoying the view along the way, and self-discovery, itself, comes through self-observation. Our feelings, good or bad, resourceful or not, are not the master of our lives, they are only experiences, nothing more, nothing less, just experiences. We are the masters of our lives, and our success will be followed by our own self-discovery. Our happiness comes from us, not at us. What we accomplish or what we have in our lives should make no difference in maintaining our level of happiness. True happiness is total freedom to be who we are and what we were meant to be.

"Happiness only happens in this moment, love only operates in the present," I said, interrupting the silence, "without a past or future. If we stay focused on the present, the future will take care of itself. We plan for the future by how we take care of the present, and by living in the present, you send love into your future and you heal your past. Happiness is being lonely or having a loving relationship. Happiness is being sick or being healthy. Happiness is being broke or having money. Happiness has to be whatever we are going through at the moment. We are not our past or our future. If we can live in the present where the action is, where happiness and love are always there, that is where we will find our true self. Not at the end of the path but on the journey itself. So, then, does it matter which path we take?"

"Just as long as there are a few trees to hug along the way, it probably makes little difference," Weston replied giving me a less than gentle punch on my arm. "Race you to the trailer we call home." And off he ran.

Accepting the challenge, I was right behind him in pursuit. As we neared the trailer I saw the car pull into the driveway, and heard the car door slam. Walker was home.

"Dad," I heard him yell as he ran toward me. "Boy, am I glad you're home."

In his arms he carried three books. "All these books are about rattlesnakes. I'm going to learn all about them and then help them find a new home," his voice was filled with that same excitement I had heard on the phone. "Come and sit down here in the chair so I can show you what I've got."

Joanna wasn't far behind him. "I can see you have some important stuff to discuss so I'll ask you about your seminar later." We exchanged kisses and then she handed me two more books about rattlesnakes before stepping into the trailer.

Weston was leaning against the trailer when I reached the chair, a look of victory shining in his eyes. "Not bad for a man your age," he sympathized. He patted the chair and motioned for me to sit.

Walker pulled a chair close to mine, quickly made himself comfortable, and opened the first book. We found ourselves staring at bugging eyes staring back at us. I shuttered as I thought of the rattlesnake I had encountered just the week before. It looked just like this one. In fact they all looked just like the one I had encountered just different colors.

"The lady at the library told me that there are more than eighty living species of rattlesnakes," Walker explained as he turned to a page that had been marked by the librarian. "In California there's four main ones, the Sidewinder and Red Diamond rattlesnakes," Walker pointed to pictures of each as he pronounced their names.

The picture of the Sidewinder showed indents in the sand left by the snake as it slithered demonstrating the side maneuver. The Red Diamond, pictured in living color left no doubt as to why it was so named.

"Then there's the Speckled Panamint and Western Diamond Back rattlesnakes," he continued as he turned to the page showing two more pictures. The Diamond Back, the diamond-shaped markings showing along the back of its scaled skin, was coiled in the shade of a rock. The picture of the Panamint was taken from a distance, however, making it difficult to identify any specific markings. I wondered if the fact the picture was not a close-up had significant meaning.

In our haste to eliminate our foe we had failed to identify those who called our home, their own. I'm glad Walker had the foresight to want to study the predators and learn more about them before tangling with them.

Our first encounter with a rattler had been a month ago. I was driving home from a business trip and was still about a hundred miles away when my cell phone rang. Joanna was on the other end.

"We've got a problem," she breathed into the phone, her voice shaking.

All sorts of things were whizzing through my mind. Something had happened to one of the kids, the house, the dog. "What is it?" I was almost frantic. Here I was stuck in traffic a hundred miles from home.

"There is a rattle snake basking in the sun on the top step of the trailer," she cried, "and we can't get out."

Relieved in the fact that the problem wasn't as serious as I first envisioned, I asked, "Have you tried pushing the screen door against it?"

"That didn't work. We've even tried throwing things at it. It refuses to budge. What do I do now?"

"Do you have access to a phone?"

"Obviously, I'm talking to you."

"Right." Traffic can do that to you when you are trying to get home, I decided. "Call the neighbor closest to us, David, and explain the situation. I'm sure he will come over and take care of it," I suggested. "And, Joanna, call me right back. I'm still ninety-five miles away."

Twenty minutes later the phone rang again. Joanna's voice was much more calm this time.

"David, the neighbor came right over with his BB gun and shot it in the head to stun it," she said, "then, he took it away, I suppose, to kill it away from the boys."

"I'll be home in less than an hour, Joanna, and I'll personally thank David," I said, relief lifting the tension in my body. "Are you alright?"

"I'm fine now."

"Good, I'll see you then." The road was clear ahead of me and I had made good time.

I wonder, now, what kind of rattler it was and how it had found its way to our front steps. I thought snakes, especially rattlers sought seclusion and that they preferred the shade to the sun. Walker's idea to study and understand them better had been pure genius.

"I'm going to study these books and learn all about the snakes so I can help them find a new home, far away from here, then mom won't be scared," Walker said as he was about to close the book.

"Wait," Weston's voice startled Walker and he jumped, nearly dropping all the books on his lap. "Look at those round holes underneath the eyes. What are they?"

Walker handed the book to Weston who read the words underneath the picture explaining the 'pits'. "Can you believe this," he said. "They are heat sensors. They're heat-radiation-detecting organs used as a homing device enabling the rattlesnake to 'see' warm blooded animals…like us."

"Really?" Walker's eyes were the size of silver dollars. "Cool."

"They use them to find their prey at night or in dark hiding places. They can spot a mouse and judge the distance to ensure an accurate strike from as far away as two feet." Weston continued to read. "When the pits are directed upward, they act as a final homing device if the prey should move during the strike."

"Can't they see?" I asked, wanting to get in on the conversation.

"It says here," Weston said after locating the page that described the eyes, "that they can't see very clearly but can differentiate size, shape, light and shadow. But because their eyes are set toward the sides of the head, they have elliptical pupils, giving them better overall vision."

"What does elliptical mean?" asked Walker.

"Elliptical is a path of a point that moves so that the sum of its distances from two fixed points remains the same." I explained.

"Huh?" he exclaimed.

"It means they're oval," Weston interceded. "It also says here that snakes don't have movable eyelids, that inside the eye the lens is focused by moving it forward and backward like a camera lens."

"Cool," whispered Walker

"Cool," I echoed.

"I wonder what it says about their tongues," Walker said as he picked up another book and began to search through its pages. "Here, look!" He pointed to a picture showing the tongue as it protruded through slits in a snake's mouth. "Here, read it, Dad," he requested as he handed me the book.

I began to read. "The tongue is forked and is called the Jacob's Organ. It is a collector of a sensory apparatus found within paired cavities in the roof of the mouth. The tongue discerns chemical information about its surroundings. Also, the tongues of different snakes are different colors."

"How come our tongues don't have a sensory organ?" Walker asked.

"Because our eyes and ears have them," Weston answered. "And, besides we would look funny going around with our tongues hanging out." He couldn't resist, at that point, giving a full demonstration.

We laughed as we mocked Weston. The noise brought the dog barking, her tongue hanging as she skidded to a stop in front of my chair. There we all stood, our tongues protruding staring at each other looking as if our sanity was in question. Joanna shouted behind us and we turned toward the trailer just in time to hear the snap of the camera she held in her hands.

"A picture for posterity," she remarked, acknowledging that our sanity was intact. "Now I think it is time to wash your hands before dinner."

I watched as the boys gathered the books in their arms and disappeared inside the trailer. There goes love, I thought as I recalled Weston's words earlier when he said the trailer wasn't anything until we filled it with our love.

Joanna, looking stern but unable to hide the amusement in her eyes, made one request at the dinner table "I think I would like to eat this whole meal without hearing the word, *snake*. Everyone agree?"

"Agreed," everyone chorused, and dinner was served.

Three hours later when the boys were in bed, I took my journal outside and sat in my lounge chair, a very comfortable, perfectly padded reclining chair, which I actually get to sit in when no one else is around. Joanna soon joined me, however, so reluctantly I asked if she would like me to move so she could sit in my chair. To my relief she

declined my offer to move but accepted the invitation of the chair and cuddled up next to me.

"I've been thinking," I said, as I put my arm around her, "that dealing with a rattlesnake is like dealing with anger."

"How romantic." she sighed, leaning her head on my shoulder and closing her eyes. "I now see my mistake in not including the whole evening in my request at dinner,"

I pretended not to notice her reluctance to be a part of this discussion and asked, "Have you ever thought how being close to a snake is like being close to anger?"

"Not recently," she yawned.

"Think about the instructions we've given the boys. What are they to do if they encounter a rattlesnake?" I prodded

"Do you want an answer right away?" She opened one eye as she asked the question.

"I'll give you two minutes to repeat the instructions," I laughed.

"I can see you are serious about this so let me recite them to you, but I get to do it with my eyes shut. Ok?"

"Fair enough." I conceded.

"First, if they can hear it that means it is close. They need to be observant and locate the snake then decide its distance. If it is too close, they are to stand still. Otherwise they are to back away slowly and quietly. If, by chance, it does bite, they are to remain calm and walk, not run, to the house and let one of us know what has happened so we can get them to the doctor for the antidote. How did I do?"

"You get those four silver stars," I said, pointing toward the sky in the direction of the big dipper. "We'll just keep them up there so they won't get lost and you can see them whenever you want any time after sunset and we are in the lounge chair like we are right now."

"That's what I like about you," she opened her eyes and winked, "Even while you are deep in universal thoughts you really can be romantic. Now give me your theory on rattlesnakes and anger."

"Think about what you said. First you hear, then you observe. After which you have to decide which to do, stand still or step away. Whatever you do, it's imperative that you remain calm. You walk, don't run and stay emotionally in the game. If, by chance, you get bitten then you request the antidote.

Wouldn't anger be handled very much the same? If you can hear the angry person, you need to observe where the anger is coming from. Then you decide how close you are to the source of the anger. Are you too close and must stand still, surrounded by the anger, or are you far enough away that you can back away from it? If, by chance you must feel the bite, then calmly walk towards help and receive the antidote."

"But, what is the antidote for anger?" Joanna asked, raising her head, her eyes searching mine.

"Patience and tolerance, simply patience and tolerance," I replied. "We have to realize, of course, that every individual has a different truth from which they view the situation. That truth will dictate how they apply tolerance and patience, determine the outcome if they proceed, then how they take action."

"What if there is no action to take?"

"If there is no action to take, just simply walk away."

"That might work," she said as she lifted herself out of the lounge chair. "Now open that journal and write while I go in and prepare a special antidote for cuddling under the stars." With those words she reached down, kissed me gently on the lips and disappeared into the trailer. I was going to discuss Peru with her but that can wait until tomorrow.

I pulled the chair in upright position as our dog Bella found a spot beside me, her nose nuzzling my shoe and I asked myself, *why am I so happy?* The answer is, because it's a good day to have lived.

Today, not only did I learn a little bit more about love, gratitude, and the magic of clouds, but I was also reminded that nature has a melody, and that paths are taken not for the reward at the end, but for the discoveries made along the way. And, today, I also learned a few important facts about snakes.

I pulled my pen from my pocket and opened the journal. I couldn't put the last words Joanna had spoken before she entered the trailer, aside, so I let the feeling they left inside me guide me as I wrote. It didn't take long to write the things I wanted to remember about this day. I closed the journal and whispered goodnight to the four stars I had given to Joanna, gave them a last look and went into the trailer.

REFLECTIONS

Journal Entry

Even though the night is warm, the chair feels cool without Joanna cuddled beside me. We take so much for granted each day.

> *We expect the stars to be our guide.*
> *The sun to keep us warm.*
> *We expect Love to stand beside us*
> *And protect us from the storm.*

Why do I feel so happy? Let's see, to be happy means to be content, fortunate, pleased. I am all of these. But I think happiness means even more than that.

> *Happiness is not what we have but what we give.*
> *The homeless man, in need of food,*
> *And a child with the heart to give,*
> *Are both rewarded.*

> *Happiness is not where we live, but how we live,*
> *Like the old oak tree with roots sunk deep,*
> *To weather the storm*
> *It is the welcome voice of home.*

WHAT I HAVE LEARNED FROM MY SIX SONS

Happiness is not rewards at the end,
but discoveries along the way.
Both the good and the bad
For if we learn nothing about ourselves,
We learn nothing at all.

Happiness is not in the past or the future, but in the present.
Like a cloud molded and transformed,
Through the rays of the sun,
It comes from us not at us.

Happiness is Hugging a tree
It's good for the soul

Happiness is taking a walk in nature
It's feeling the earth beneath your feet

Happiness is listening.
It's good for the mind

Happiness is understanding
It's good for the heart.

Happiness is a child who cares about snakes.

Why am I so happy? Because it has been a good day to have lived. Oh, one more thing. Happiness is being able to share my philosophy on anger and snakes with someone who will listen, even if it is with her eyes shut.

Thought for Today

Everyone is searching for the correct path to truth,
While the real truth is,
there is no correct path,
except the one we create ourselves.

Chapter Five

I woke to the memory of a dog, three boys and a man who had never had the chance to be boy, doing a comical impression of a snake. I liked the feeling of freedom that came with being a child or in my case, being as a child. I found myself on a natural 'high'. It was a good feeling.

I took some time to recall my own childhood and with recollection came mixed emotions. My parents had been all they knew how to be, giving all they had to give. I realize that now, as an adult, though I didn't at the time. Now I thank my parents every day in my heart for all they taught me and the love they shared with me and my three siblings.

My memories of a father in life and then in death are vivid. He was a quiet man. I will never know what he felt inside as he struggled to provide for us. I don't recall my father ever complaining about the cards he'd been dealt, I only remember him doing whatever work he could find to support his family. I would give anything to be able to sit with him now and listen to the story of his life that was never told.

What moved my father? What heartaches and pains did he keep locked inside? What were his dreams and aspirations that went unfulfilled? What made him happy? There is so much I don't know about him but I do know that I felt the strength of his love for me many times as I was growing up, and that carried me through the hard times.

The day he died I sat by his hospital bed, holding his hand as he drifted in and out of consciousness, tears rolling down my cheeks. I wanted to tell him how much I loved him. I wanted to thank him for everything he had done for me. I wanted him to know that because he taught me to work, to keep going even when my hands were bleeding from picking cotton, and my back felt like it was breaking, I had become the success of his example. It dawned on me then, I was more like my father than I thought. We both had kept the secrets of our feelings tucked inside.

In the final moments we had together, I leaned down to him and carefully wrapped him in my arms, knowing it would be for the last time, and as I did I heard the quick, quiet breaths of a sob escape his chest and I knew he was trying to tell me he loved me, but that it was time for him to go now.

His eyes opened as he reached up and wiped away the tear that escaped from inside. Then he closed his eyes again and went peacefully to sleep, for the last time. I knew he was free, and the joy I felt for him pushed aside the pain in my heart as I kissed him gently on the forehead and whispered good-bye.

I couldn't let go of his hand, I didn't want to sever the connection yet. I didn't want to take my eyes from his face. I hadn't expected the serenity I found there and I knew at that moment I had finally met the man I never really knew in life, the man he was deep inside, and my heart wept.

"When you were a child," I whispered to myself, "did you play as a child? Did you and your father run and laugh together like I do with my sons, or was your childhood filled with responsibilities beyond your years as mine was?"

As I looked in his face I tried to envision him as a child, climbing trees and catching lightning bugs in a jar. I could almost picture him playing hide-n-seek, eating his mother's fresh baked cookies, and going fishing. As I allowed my imagination to take me into his boyhood, I could see him walking on stilts and shooting a sling shot, chewing gum in school and buying penny candy. I watched him eat banana splits and play marbles for keeps. And I think he listened to the Lone Ranger on the radio and drank cherry cokes at the corner drug store.

The thoughts of what his childhood might have been brought the warmth of peace, and though I will never know because I never asked, I truly believe he did do those things and that I was allowed a glimpse into his life. Thinking about my father today brought a renewed feeling of respect for his life and his love.

I could hear Walker shouting, and Bella barking outside and I remembered another time when Walker was three and Will was five. I had been an innocent observer of the game they were playing, when suddenly I found myself skipping around the tree with them. Walker had simply looked up at me in total acceptance of a playmate and said, "Hi Jimmy," and grabbed my hand while Will grabbed the other.

One day I taught them to make fishing poles, and showed them which worms made the best bait. Another day we built tunnels in the ground together, tunnels big enough to crawl through. These things I had learned from my father, and probably he had learned them from his father.

"Hey Dad," Will's voice came from the hall. "Can you give me a ride to soccer practice?"

I slipped the thoughts of my father into the back of my mind. "Sure, I'm going to grab an apple," I called back, "then I'll meet you at the car."

I love to get into a car with Will. He loves to talk. He loves to share things and ask questions. I needed that this morning and I was not disappointed.

He was waiting in the car when I got there, his shin guards resting on his lap, the bill of his red baseball cap shading his eyes and his favorite ball propped between his knees. He looked the part of a serious soccer player, but as we were driving down the road he said, "Dad, do you know why we have monkeys on earth?"

I looked at him and knew beneath the facade was still the boy who loved to talk. "No, why?" I asked, relieved in the knowledge.

"I think it's to keep the banana population down."

It was difficult for me to keep from laughing, however, I couldn't think of a better reason.

"You know what?" he continued without hardly stopping for a breath.

"What?" I asked again, my interest peaking now.

"I think I was born to be wet."

"Ah," I replied, beginning to understand why he was always pouring water on himself, why he would be jumping up and down on the trampoline with the hose shooting water in the air. It was all very clear now, he was born to be wet.

As he climbed out of the car and waved his goodbye, I recalled another time when he had climbed out of the car for baseball practice just a few years ago and I had overheard him tell his coach. "You know I am not a runner, I don't run."

"Is that a fact?" I watched a cheerful smile appear on the coach's face as he spoke.

"Yes," Will continued, "so you need to put me in one place."

During that year he had spent a lot of time out in the field where he often sat cross legged picking at the flowers. At the end of that season he informed his coach that he was retiring from baseball.

Today he has become a runner and a start soccer player. There is nothing like maturity to change a guy.

As I watched him walk toward the field, I had a distinct and unwavering feeling move through me, and I could sense more than see someone familiar walking with him. It was as if time had been altered for a brief moment and was allowing me a glimpse of the connection between two souls that time, itself, could not sever. I got out of the car and made my way toward the field where Will was laughing with the other boys. I glanced quickly around wishing I could explain to myself, what or who it was I was looking for. I could see no one. Disappointed, yet not knowing why I felt such disappointment, I settled back into the seat of my car, wishing I could understand the feeling of love that enveloped my soul. I wish Michael were here to explain it to me.

Two hours later, when I picked Will up from practice he climbed in the car, a broad smile on his face, his hair wet with perspiration and the clothes that were clean when he got out of the car a few hours earlier, were now streaked with dirt and mud. He placed the soccer ball on his lap and the shin guards in the floor and calmly said, "Made two goals in practice and one from mid field. Both of them were amazing. I'm going to do the same thing in the game on Wednesday. Will you be here to see it?"

"Wouldn't miss it," I answered, making a mental note to check my calendar to see if there was anything I would have to cancel in order to be there. "Anybody watching your practice today?" I asked casually,

"Nope, but I sure had a good practice," his eyes were bright with enthusiasm.

We rode in silence for almost two minutes before he spoke again. "What do you think about, Dad, when you don't have to think about anything?" He asked as he rolled the window down to let the breeze dry his hair.

I thought for a moment then replied, "You know, Will, I have never really thought about that. I guess I'll have to do some thinking before I can answer your question."

He giggled, then he continued. "You know what I think about? I think about gentle things. I think about things that don't need to be worried about. But most of the time I think about us and being a family, and about God."

"Those are wonderful things to think about when you don't have to think," I said, touched by his insight. "Perhaps if more people thought about things like that the world would be a better place."

"Want to know what else I think?" he asked.

"Yes, I do," I answered honestly.

"I think moms and grandmas should run the world," his voice becoming more serious now. "There wouldn't be any wars because mom's won't let you fight and grandmas won't let you get hurt. Grandmas would make everybody talk to each other and play jump rope together and color together and make cookies together. Then moms would make everybody clean up the mess together. Wouldn't it be great, everyone would know everyone else and, you know what Dad, we are all made just the same, because God made us all."

I love the wisdom of this child. What could we, in this world, accomplish, if before going to war, governments would listen to the voices of the children. There is peace in a child's wisdom, tolerance in a child's love. Therein the harmony of justice and the rhythm of freedom could create a rich melody so incredibly pure that it would reach the core of the inner cities, shoot its music throughout the veins of the world until, finally, in its vibrato burst through the universe. The music of the universe. If we could only hear it, what would we feel. Perhaps we would feel a little more like children.

"I wish you were President," I smiled as we pulled into the temporary driveway.

"Look, Dad, there's a worker at the new house," Will said with excitement in his voice. "Maybe they are going to work on our house again."

I could see the contractor's truck parked by the unfinished house. He was talking to Joanna and she was smiling. That was a good sign that work was going to commence once again.

Will ran into the trailer to clean up and I quickly found my way to Joanna's side just in time to hear the contractor say that his crew would be here Monday morning at 8:00. In the meantime, he wanted to come out and walk through the changes with us. He unrolled the blueprints on the floor and kneeling on one knee, bent over them, then glanced toward a window frame. He took out his measuring tape and handed me one end and stretched it across to the frame, noted that the window in the new blueprint was in the correct place. Next was the door. The adjustment of eight inches for the wall had been made. He gathered the blueprints up and walked through the house, checking each change indicated.

"OK," he said as he walked toward us, rolling up the blueprints, "everything seems in order, we'll see you on Monday." He waved as he climbed into his truck and drove away from the property.

"He thinks it will be done in six to eight weeks," laughed Joanna, as she wrapped her arms around my waist and swung me into a slow waltz on the floor of what will be the dining room.

"By the way," I said, as we danced our way into the living room, "Will thinks it would be a good idea if you ran the country."

"Not until my castle is finished could I even consider taking on the country," she curtsied as she spoke. "For now I must concentrate on controlling the rattlesnakes, howbeit, thy son, Walker, has come forth with a solution you might consider."

I looked into the beautiful eyes of this woman I had married and considered myself a lucky man.

We walked back to the trailer arm in arm and I opened the door for Joanna, then kissed her hand and bowed before her. "I shall go in search of my son, my lady."

She gracefully turned and stepping across the threshold, "You will find him by the oak tree with a book in his hand," she said as she dismissed me with the wave of her hand.

I could see Walker as I neared the old oak. He was sitting cross-legged among the leaves, his right arm supporting his head as his arm rested on his knee, his hand against his cheek. A book lay open on his lap and I could hear him reading out loud while the sunlight bounced its rays off the top of his head. Bella was lying beside him, watching his face, her ears perked as if she were listening to every word. I just stood there wishing I had a camera to immortalize this captive scene. I thought of my friend at the airport, C.T., and his sketchbook. He would have captured the mood in the picture even better than a camera.

I stood there wanting to let the scene play itself out undisturbed but Bella's bark told me she had spotted me. Walker's eyes lifted from the page and looked in my direction. "Dad," he called, "there is some really neat stuff in this book. I'll tell you all about it."

I settled myself beside him and rested my back against the tree. "I'm ready to listen," I said.

Walker's eyes were bright with excitement. "Snakes haven't got any outside ear openings," he began. "So they can't hear very good, and they don't have to sniff for their food like dogs cause they have smelling cells in their noses that are really sensitive." He paused taking a deep breath. "You'll never believe this, but rattlesnakes have from one hundred and sixty to four-hundred pairs of ribs and don't have a sternum, that's the name of the bone we have right here on our chest," he said as he pointed to his sternum. "The ribs curve around the snake's body and that's how it keeps its shape."

"You have uncovered some very interesting facts in your research," I said, "please go on."

"Well, their skin bends really easy and they have scales on their skin that makes it tough but they can still feel anything that touches them, no matter how soft. They have things called touch sensors all over their bodies, even in between the little things called scales. The snake's skin tells it what the temperature is and that is really important to a snake."

Bella had lost interest in our conversation and had found something much more to her taste like chasing a squirrel up a tree. We were left to discuss snakes on our own.

"Did you know that snakes don't chew their food, they just swallow whatever they put in their mouths, like a bird or a lizard, or a frog and even bigger animals like gophers and rabbits and squirrels." He stopped talking and gave me a comical look. "I don't think Mom would let them eat at our table." he laughed.

Walker closed the book and set it on the grass, retrieving another one in which he had placed a bookmark. Handing it to me he said, "Here Dad, you need to read this because it tells us how we can help the snakes find a new home."

I turned to the page that had been marked and quickly scanned it. "*Unlike many snake species,*" I began to read, " *rattlesnakes rarely choose to live near human habitations. They prefer natural, undisturbed areas.* That's good to know." I chuckled. "Maybe we should have our snakes read this part."

"See what it says next." Walker urged.

"*If rattlesnakes are known to be in the vicinity of a house, certain precautions will make the home site less suitable for the snakes.*" The book now had my full attention. "It says here," I said as I studied the page, "that rattlesnakes are attracted by food, and what we need to do is eliminate their source of food around the property. That would mean any small rodent." My eyes moved from the page to the small forest around me and I began to calculate how many different species of rodents we supported on our land.

"Not only rodents, Dad, but other things too like covering trash cans and cleaning out the vegetable gardens," he prompted." And moving things like woodpiles, rock piles, and keeping the grass cut short. We just need to get rid of anything that will make them want to stay."

"It says here that they always follow the same path so all we need to do is mount up and cut them off at the path." I remarked with a touch of a western drawl.

Walker's face lit up with laughter and Bella, who's ears have acute radar, came running at the sound, and pawed her way between us. Her tongue found Walker's cheek while his arms found their way around her neck. As boy and dog came together, the impact sent them rolling and down they went in continual motion until they reached the tree and its huge roots blocked their progress. The strains of their frivolous delight filled the air and I knew why God made children so innocent and dogs so loyal.

What a picture they presented as they made their way back to where I sat, the dog in the lead, and I wished again I had a camera in my pocket. Walker's hair was rumpled, and adorned with dry leaves and tiny sticks. Dead grass had attached itself to his clothes and his face was dusted with natures powder. Bella? Well at this point Bella could have passed for his twin.

Walker brushed himself off and dropped down in front of me while Bella shook her coat vigorously, sending leaves and dust over the books, my pants and my shirt, then wiggled her way between us. That brought a giggle from Walker and an apologetic whimper from the dog. I had to giggle too as I reached over and brushed the lingering debris from Walker's hair and I felt the child in myself squirm with the desire to be set free.

Just as it had earlier, a warm feeling passed through me again, and I suddenly felt the sensation of another man sitting there, laughing with us. It was as if there was a space between thought where I connected to source, free of expectations and attachments. I sensed a feeling of total peace, as if a connection had been made between two souls, mine and his, and I felt his joy and his love. I sensed his approval not only of who I had become, but of the father I had become. I sensed his love for Walker now as I had sensed his love for Will as he walked with him to the soccer field earlier. I glanced at Walker and he smiled at me and winked. It all seemed so natural to him.

This morning, as I thought about my father, there was such an aching in my heart. Had my longing to know him better brought him to me? Had Walker and Will been the conduit through which the message was transferred? Where they his messengers?

An emotional surge ignited me and I wanted to run over to where I had felt the man's presence and put my arms around him. I wanted him to answer all the questions I held inside. I wanted to ask about my mother, but even as these questions entered my mind, it was as if they were answered. The questions simply drifted away and in their place a feeling of such tremendous acceptance and unconscious love filled my heart, and the aching was gone. My heart held only answers now and I knew my mother and father were together and they were happy beyond anything I could comprehend. My heart pounded with the hope that he might stay a little longer but as quickly as the connection had come, it was gone.

That day in the hospital, after my father died, I had wanted desperately to feel the presence of his spirit in the room. The room, however, remained quiet and empty, and I could feel nothing. But today I felt something that can't be explained with simple words. My father had come to share this timeless moment with me, and though we didn't speak of it, Walker and I had traveled to the center of love.

"Now, where were we?" I heard Walker say in a sober tone that contradicted the smile he couldn't hide, and he brought my attention back to the rattlesnakes

"I'm not sure," I asked, and we were back as if nothing had happened. But something had happened and it would remain with me forever.

"We were mounting up," Walker laughed.

"That's right. Let's see the rest of the page explains how to build a drift fence. It can be made of anything that will block the snake's passage completely. The snake would just follow the course of the fence. It doesn't have to be any more than three feet high but it has to fit closely to the ground or be buried one to two inches."

"Wow!" he almost shouted as his eyes widened. "That's a lot of fence, isn't it, Dad." We have ten acres!

"What do you think we should do?"

"I think we had better try to help them find a new home," he said with intent, "because their venom is very important to people. I know that sounds funny when you know that it can kill you, but scientists have been studying it and they think it has something in it that can help cure some diseases that can also kill people." He turned the page and pointed to a paragraph. "Read this."

I began to read, *A nerve growth-promoting factor has been segregated in the venom of some rattlesnake species. This has opened new doors and accelerated research into the complexities of diseases that produce permanent nerve damage, such as multiple sclerosis and Alzheimer's disease.*

"They don't kill the snakes to get the venom, Dad, they milk them. You know something else?" he continued, "Rattlesnakes and buffalo lived together in Western Oklahoma for thousands of years, and it was not the snakes that killed almost all of the buffalo, man did that."

"And did you read all about this by yourself?" I asked, knowing his reading ability wasn't quite advanced at this level of study.

"You know I can't read those big words, Dad," he laughed. "But Mom can and she read this book to me and we discussed all this stuff already."

I was amazed he had remembered 'all this stuff' he and Joanna had read together. He is really serious about helping these snakes, so I better be serious about helping him.

As we continued to study the book and idea struck me, "Maybe we should call in a specialist to trap the snakes and take them away until we can have a drift fence built," I heard myself say. Had I developed, over the past several minutes, a respect of a predator I consider an enemy? That they could be a service to mankind had never occurred to me. Still, I would be very apprehensive if I came upon one coiled in its own defense, but my education has given me a better understanding of my opponent.

"Could we do that for now, Dad?" He asked as he turned to the last page of the book." Look, on this page it tells about some people who are working to help the rattlesnakes and there's a number to call." Walker's commitment was visible, "I'm going to call and get some information then I'll tell you what they said."

"In the meantime," I asked, "If I encounter one can I kill it?"

"Of course, Dad," he replied, a serious look on his face, "You're much more important than a rattlesnake."

"Thank you." I breathed a sigh of relief.

We gathered up the books and headed back toward the trailer. As we came to the unfinished house I excused myself because I wanted to check some measurements before Monday. Walker waved his hand then yelled to his dog and off they ran.

As I walked through what would be the kitchen area of the house I found myself drifting back to the experience under the oak tree, then I thought about the word, "Resourceful"- where all things originate. To know this spot, whatever it may be referred to as, is to know who you are, not by name or identity, but by the deep feeling of connectedness where we know our place in connection to the infinite. Perhaps that's where we communicate with loved ones already passed.

I believe this is the place where life begins and ends, but because we all live in a place of ongoing tension of the world, in time we become tarnished or covered over by life itself. When we break through the film that living life has created, we experience moments of enlightenment, moments of wholeness, moments of clear thinking and feeling. When the real inner core of our being meets with the outer physical being, we experience moments of complete oneness. Whether we experience this connectedness during a moment of trauma, or simply sitting under an oak tree with a child, it doesn't really matter. That timeless spot of grace and oneness is the ultimate goal.

Regardless of the vehicle or the subject taught, how to uncover that original center and how to live in that place more often is really the only thing worth teaching.

Sitting there under the oak tree with Walker and, in my heart knowing that my father was there, opened my mind to all this that I believe. Why would I question what I witnessed? Why should I try to explain to myself what I already know?

Having that all settled in my mind, I went in search for the well-traveled path between the house and the trailer. As I walked I would turn to look at the house, trying to imagine it finished.

I had gone maybe fifty feet when I thought I saw movement in the underbrush, and an eerie feeling came over me that there was a snake nearby. Could I have imagined it, after all I had just been reading about them and looking at very life-like and vivid pictures. The feeling, however, did not lift and I became more alert as I continued to walk. All of a sudden, I heard a crunching sound and as I slowly turned my head to the right, a pair of huge snake eyes glared at me and my hair all but stood on end. I forgot all the good things I had just read about them, self-preservation was the only thing on my mind.

The kitchen window of the trailer was opened and I could see Joanna near it, so with as much intensity as I could muster, I yelled to her to bring me the shovel. Joanna wasted no time as she could see my dilemma from where she stood and within seconds I had a shovel in my hands.

The snake was about six feet long. The shovel was about five feet long. Not wanting to get any closer to the snake than I already was, I aimed the shovel, shut my eyes and visualized hitting the snake. I threw the shovel and when I opened my eyes I had severed its head. It had died without moving. Joanna and I stood there speechless, staring at the snake until I could thaw my body enough to pick up the shovel and scoot the remains of a once deadly Diamond Back into the underbrush until I could make better arrangements.

Joanna took my hand and we walked back to the trailer together. I was grateful I had made a deal with Walker that I could still kill a snake if I encountered it for now.

"I think I'll give you a '10' on the throw," - Joanna broke the silence, her voice was still a little shaky, but her sense of humor was intact. "Considering your eyes were shut at the time."

"I'm just glad I had permission from Walker to defend myself against them until further notice." I laughed as I explained what we had talked about as I studied the library books with him.

I wanted, with all my heart, to tell Joanna of my remarkable experience under the oak tree. I wanted to share the sensitivity of the impression I felt as I witnessed the presence. I wanted to tell her how my heart wept when I thought of my father this morning and of the overwhelming love I feel for him today. I wanted to ask if she thought it possible that my father wanted me to know something too, and this was his way of connecting, but the words wouldn't come. So, for now I would keep it wrapped safely in my heart.

When I reached my lounge chair, in front of the trailer, I fell into it like a rag doll. My heart still pounding and my knees weak.

"I think you need some time out," Joanna said softly. "Take a nap, you deserve it."

Putting the snake out of my mind, I closed my eyes and took a deep breath, then slipped my way into a depth of stillness, like the diver experiences as he sinks beneath the churning of the waves. I began to mediate on the things I do that make me feel truly connected and alive. I thought of playing with my boys, reading, an intimate dinner with Joanna, making love with her, exercising, writing, being in nature, fishing, doing nothing, and vowed to do each of them more often.

Reflections

Journal entry

With death comes recognition of a person's life. Only when it's too late do we find we are void of answers to the questions that dwell in our hearts. We are filled with all the words unspoken and an emptiness invades where there can be no replies. Why is it so?

We are connected with this world
Through an awareness that comes with birth.
And an acceptance that comes with death
That is life.

We are connected one with another,
When we share the laughter of joy,
And the tears of sorrow
That is love.

WHAT I HAVE LEARNED FROM MY SIX SONS

Each generation gives to the next in one-way or the other. My father taught me, and what I learned from him, I taught my sons. They, in turn, will teach their children.

It is so subtle,
We watch.
And without knowing,
We learn.
And without knowing,
We become.

I owe my sons,
The wisdom
Of my father,
Who learned wisdom
From his father
And so on.

I owe my son
The time
To listen to him so,
In time,
He will listen,
To me.

I wonder if all parents feel the way I do, about their children? I think we would all agree it isn't easy to be a parent, but it has the greatest rewards.

I think the best baseball players are under five feet.
I think the world would be a better place if we would listen more and talk less.
I think the world should be in the hands of grandmothers who bake cookies and like to color.
I think a house takes a long time to build.
I think little boys and dogs belong together.
I think rattlesnakes do have their place it just isn't on my land.
I think I am glad I'm more important than a rattlesnake.
I think love can make miracles.
I think reading and playing and meditating should be a part of every day
I think making love is a glimpse of eternity and experience the deepest connection.
And I think that once in a while it's good to just do nothing.

Thought for Today

If we want to see how well we've done in our lives,
all we need to do is watch our children.
They are our greatest success.

Chapter Six

I think it is common knowledge that when you pray for patience, it is served to you on a silver platter of impatience. Things make you impatient so you can let go of them. You can't have patience when you have impatience. There is not room for both. The same goes with love. You can't have love when you are filled with non-love.

I had just written this statement on a piece of paper when I glanced out the window in time to see Walker run past with his dog. As I watched him I remembered a little boy, not yet old enough to express himself vocally but with pure love he wraps his arms around my neck and squeezes tight. I hold him just as tight, not wanting to ever let go for fear he will run outside and grow up and we will never have this moment again.

In my heart I ask, "My sweet child, what are you here to teach me?" and in my heart he answers, "I'm here to teach you that I love you." The next thing I knew, he ran outside and grew up.

I watched as he threw a stick high into the air for his dog to chase, his blond hair dancing in the breeze. He was wearing Will's old sweat shirt and a pair of shorts. He insisted long pants slowed him down. He had on a pair of slip-on tennis shoes so he didn't have to waste time with laces or Velcro.

He was laughing, the dog was barking and I was trying not to cry. I watched how patient he was with his dog and how patient his dog was with him.

Walker's six years has been full of clear intention that he can do anything he sets his mind to do.

When he was four, he came to me and said, "Dad, in the gym I go to, there is a rope, twenty-four feet long, that goes to the ceiling and on the ceiling there's a bell. The coach says the first one to climb the rope and ring the bell gets a gold medal."

Knowing that kids up to the age of twelve went to the gym, I inquired. "Has anyone come close to ringing the bell yet?"

"Nope, not yet. I've tried a few times but only made it part way," he said and off he ran to play.

I had all but forgotten the conversation when one morning he announced to me. "Today, I'm going to the top."

"What do you mean, you're going to the top?" I asked as I fluffed his hair.

"I'm going to the top of the rope when I go to the gym this morning," he said, intention showing in his face.

I looked at Walker thinking, that's a lot of determination for such a small boy. Would it be enough, so I said to him, "Tell me how are you going to do that."

He looked at me not wavering, "I don't know yet, but I'm going to."

I knelt so that we were almost eye-to-eye and I said, "You just step back and look at that rope, spit in both hands and rub them together then go to the top and ring the bell."

He nodded as if he knew that was what he had to do, and, then, he put his little hands on each side of my face and pulled my face close to his until our noses almost touched and repeated, "I'm going to the top today." With that, he released me and he was gone.

As I worked through the morning I was concerned that Walker was not yet mature enough to climb to the top. Butterflies fluttered in my stomach as my hope for his success consumed my thoughts.

Afternoon finally arrived and Walker walked into my office with a gold medal pinned to his shirt. I felt as proud as he looked.

"How did you do it?" I grinned as the butterflies quieted for a much needed rest.

"I stood at the bottom of the rope," he began, "looked at the rope and I saw myself ringing the bell. I stopped for a minute to think about it and I said to myself, I'm going to the top. I spit in both hands like you told me and rubbed them together, then I grabbed the rope and started up.

I got half way and I got tired so I stopped and then I thought, I'm going to the top. I latched on tighter and went up some more until I was almost to the top but I got tired again so I stopped and thought again, I'm going to the top." With his arms he demonstrated exactly what he had done as he spoke. "So I did and I rang the bell."

I reached out my hand and he took it with pride oozing from every inch of him. A handshake was not good enough, he needed a bear hug. He laughed and I laughed then off he ran to tell Warren.

The next day he went to the gym and went up the rope. Every day after he climbed the rope and rang the bell before doing anything else. It was simple once he had done it and he knew he could do it anytime he wanted.

It's a mind game that once you tell yourself you can do it then you can do it. Walker was not afraid to tell himself he could and then he was not afraid to do it. Once the decision was made in his mind, it was done. It reminded me of the book we all read as children, *The little Engine That Could*.

I wondered, at what point did Walker know he was ready to climb the rope? My eye caught two roses just outside my window. Joanna had planted them in a pot to be transplanted beside our new home when it is completed. Each was in a different stage of maturity as I was pondering the question in my mind. If you were to watch a flower slowly blossoming,

I thought to myself, at every passing moment it is as open as it can be. It neither pushes too hard nor holds back. The same is true with our lives. In every stage of our growth we should not expect far too much of ourselves nor should we expect much too little. If a bud were to stretch itself to be a mature flower before it was ready, it would tear or break. If we attempt to grow beyond our limits before we are mature enough, we, like the bud, would also tear and break. Our own growth, just like nature, takes time to mature. We must observe where we are in our own path, and understand that it's simply the process of blossoming, of unfolding.

Yesterday, Walker had not bloomed enough to see himself climbing the rope to the top and ringing the bell. Today, however, he was ready.

As I focused on the beauty of each rose, I view them in a new light and I vowed to never wait until some imagined end to see the beauty of my life, but rather I would appreciate the beauty of life about to open and whatever I have accomplished at the end of each day is more than enough.

"Dad," I heard Walker shout from the front yard, "It's time for the open house at school."

I looked at my watch. It was already 2:30 p.m. Though the open house went until 6:00, Walker had requested we go early. The roses were left on their own as I hurried out to the car where Joanna was waiting.

"Walker has given me specific directions as to how we are to proceed," Joanna laughed as she glanced at the instructions he had handwritten for her in crayon. "First we are to go to Will's room and go quietly to his desk and read all the things he has written, like reports and stuff. Then, we look at pictures he has colored that are hanging on the wall. After that we go to Walker's room and go quietly to his desk and follow the same procedure."

"I think we can handle that," I nodded, and when we arrived at the school we followed the instructions explicitly.

First we looked through all Will's reports and projects, inspecting each one carefully. The last paper I picked up was a report on what he was going to do when he grew up. As I reached the end of the paper I read, *The reason I want to write is because that's what my Dad does and I want to do what my Dad does.*

Joanna smiled at me as I showed her the last line. "You have a lot to live up to," she said.

"I won't mind," I said with pride.

After enjoying his artwork hanging on the wall, we went into Walker's room. As I read each paper I noticed he had written an article about the heart. The article began with, *The heart has all kinds of chambers in it and it's where your blood goes. The reason you have a pulse is to let you know that you're alive.*

"The mind of a true intellect," I said to Joanna as we enjoyed the rest of the article together.

We had walked into an elementary classroom and received an adult education, an education you can only receive by being part of a child's life.

As we drove home we talked about the conversation we had 17 years ago about having children. We both had been through the pains of divorce and we wanted to make sure what we had would last.

"What if we had decided that the risk was too great to bring children into the marriage?" I asked.

Joanna answered with another question, emotion showing in her voice, "I wonder what we would be doing today instead of driving home from an elementary school open house?" She was silent for a moment then continued, "My heart almost can't bear the thought of what we would be missing in our lives."

Joanna moved close to me, wrapped her arm through mine and laid her head on my shoulder. We didn't speak again until we pulled into the driveway.

At the end of the driveway, Will and Walker were waiting for us their faces full of anticipation. "What did you think of all the stuff we made?"

they called, almost in unison.

"We've decided we have the two smartest boys in the whole school." Joanna laughed.

"What did you like best?" Walker shouted to be heard above the dog's bark.

"Let's see," Joanna allowed her brows to furrow as if in deep thought. "I was most impressed, I think, with your report on the heart," she smiled.

"Were ya', really?" he responded proudly. "My teacher said the very same thing."

"What did ya' like best about my stuff?" cried Will, not to be outdone.

"Well, I felt so proud when I read that you wanted to be a writer because you want to be like your Dad," I felt the emotion as I spoke the words.

Both boys were beaming as they took our hands and led us back to the trailer we called home.

"I've gotta' tell you," Will said as we walked to the trailer, " Bella's been chasing the little fawn around the yard again."

As we turned the corner a frightened fawn scampered past with the dog not more than ten feet behind. I yelled at Bella but she paid no attention, she just tried to close the distance between herself and the deer.

All of a sudden a big doe jumped in front of the dog. One glance told us she was furious. Everything was moving so fast our reflexes couldn't respond. With quick speed she literally attacked Bella, her left, front hoof connecting with the dog's head, leaving a large gaping wound across her head, between her ears.

Almost by instinct, Joanna ran to the car honked the horn and scared the doe away. The scene we had witnessed left us stunned for just a second before we could run to the dog. When we reached her she was whimpering in pain and we could see she needed medical attention immediately. I gently picked her up and headed toward the car.

Will and Walker were close behind me, tears streaming down their pale faces. Joanna hurried ahead, retrieved a blanket from the trunk, placed it across the back seat, then ran back into the trailer to make a quick call to make sure a Dr. would be waiting at the vet clinic when we arrived, and to write a note to Warren and Weston, telling them what happened and where we had gone.

Will asked if he could sit by his dog so she would know how much he loved her and, without waiting for an response, he quickly climbed in the back seat beside his quivering pet.

As we hurried to the vet clinic I could hear Will speaking to Bella in soft tones. I glanced into the rear view mirror just in time to see him rub his hands together and then lay them on the dog's back. As soon as he had done this, Bella's whimpering stopped and we drove to the clinic, silence absorbed only by the sound of breathing.

While we sat, waiting for news of Bella I glanced at Will. I was amazed at the calm he brought into the room. He was holding Walker's hand and talking softly to him. We were all sitting very close together and I only had to listen to hear his words.

"You don't have to worry now, Walker, because I made him feel better with God's energy and God will make him well."

Walker lifted his tear-stained face and looked at Will. His fear was replaced with faith through the gentle words that had been spoken. He smiled at Walker and I witnessed an exchange of pure love between two brothers.

The doctor stepped into the waiting room. "I think there is a dog in there that wants to see two little boys," he said, removing the surgery cap from his head. "She is a little sleepy yet and needs to rest but she will be fine. If you will follow me."

Bella was still lying on the operating table when we entered but all signs of surgery had been removed and a colorful doggy blanket was covering her all but her head. Above her left ear, a big white bandage stood out like a beacon against her dark golden coat. The blood had been washed away leaving her coat soft and shiny.

When she heard the boys enter the room she raised her head slightly and a weak whine escaped her throat then her head was back on the table. But it was enough to let us know she was aware of our presence.

"She's a little bruised and it took 30 stitches to close all the wounds," the doctor explained, "but she will recover nicely. It's going to take some time for the wounds to heal and I'm concerned about infection so I'll give you some antibiotics to give her for ten days. Make sure she doesn't miss a dose. She will be sleepy for a few days and that's good, it will keep her inactive and give the cut more time to begin reconnecting the tissue that has been severed."

We thanked the doctor and lifted Bella back into the car and started the drive home. Both Will and Walker sat with her. She laid her head on Will's lap and her tail on Walker's.

"Is there a Dog Heaven, Dad?" asked Walker. "If Bella died would she go there?"

The answer came to me almost instantly. "Yes, Walker, there is a Heaven for dogs and Bella will go there some day, but not today."

"I'm glad." Was his only response and then he was quiet again.

Do dogs believe in God? I thought to myself. Dogs know that if you feed them at a certain time of the day, they are there at that time each day to be fed. They know love. They love their masters. They have instinct but they don't have imaginations. They don't say, *What am I going to do on Monday, or what's coming up this weekend?* At least I don't think they do. A dog just knows it's a dog by instinct and it does dog things. Dogs run around catching sticks. They chase deer and anything else that runs ahead of them without thought of consequence.

I have watched dogs play and I would think they don't have a religion nor go to church. I wonder if ants go to church. I see them marching in a very disciplined line. Their lives, therefore, must be disciplined, but do they go to church? Is there an Ant Haven? But then what do ants have to do with dogs?

Somehow, today, I know there is a place in Heaven for dogs. and that's all that matters for now.

"Remember, a long time ago, when I asked you if you knew how much I love, love, Dad?"

Will's voice broke into my thoughts.

"I remember, you said you loved love more than anything." I answered looking at him in the rear view mirror.

"And remember you asked me what love is?"

"I remember that," I continued. "You said it was getting hugs and kisses from Mom and me and your brothers, and from your grandparents and uncles and aunts.

"Love makes me love Bella too." he replied. "And love makes me miss Grandpa but someday I'll see him again in Heaven with God. Love makes me miss God too, but someday I'll be with him."

I glanced at him again through the rear view mirror and I saw a serious expression appear in his face and he spoke again. "When I thought Bella might die I felt God's love and His love is the love I like best. I knew my dog would be alright if I blessed him with God's love so I did."

There was silence in the car then, for a time, and I was reminded of another day when the feeling of love was this strong and I envisioned that winding path the minister spoke of that day as he performed our wedding ceremony. Only this time there were more than just two people walking the path, there were six and a dog.

What were the words he used? *May each one here say his or her own vow of commitment to assist Jim and Joanna in remaining true to this winding path, no matter which way it turns, knowing that they have chosen to walk it together. May they always come back to the center of the circle where they stand now together in love.*

How many times had we come back to the center of the circle? Each time we had a baby. Each time we experienced sadness or joy. And today, as we experienced with Will and Walker, the love and compassion for a dog.

The melody of a song lifted the words from my soul. *May the long-time sun shine upon you, all love surround you; may the pure light within you, guide you all the way home.*

I saw the pure light shine in two little boys and suddenly, I no longer felt sad they had to watch the attack on Bella. I believe now, there was a purpose to the event. Perhaps we needed this experience to more fully understand what we have together.

It was late when we got home and Bella was sleeping soundly. Will didn't want her to be outside, all alone, so we made her a bed with a pillow on the kitchen floor.

Warren and Weston had made some sandwiches for us so we talked for over an hour about what had happened and the feelings we had experienced.

Walker yawned then turned to Warren and explained, "there is a Dog Heaven and when Bella dies she will go there but she is not going to die today."

"That dog is not going to die for a long time, Walker," Warren laughed as he gave his younger brother a big brother's hug. "Come on, I'll help you get ready for bed before you fall asleep at the table."

"First, I have to tell Bella goodnight." Walker said and he slid from his chair and knelt by the sleeping dog on the pillow. The deep gold fur lifted and fell with each breath. The white bandage now showing traces of blood added drama to the picture and Walker let his hand travel over the spot without touching it. Then he leaned down and kissed the bandaged head ever so carefully and ran his hands through Bella's fur twice before allowing Warren to lift him up and take him into the bedroom.

Weston helped Joanna clean up the dishes while Will and I made sure there was water in the dog's dish in case she woke up during the night.

I turned down Will's bed as he changed to his pajamas. "Remember the other thing I told you that day, a long time ago?" Will asked as I tucked him into bed.

I was trying to remember the conversation, but it eluded me. "Tell me again, Will, so I will never forget."

"When I die, I don't want to be put into a box in a hole in the ground, with one of those markers on top of my head. I want to go back to God. God's love is the love I like best, so I want to be with him again someday. Don't ever forget that, Ok, Dad?"

"I will never forget that, I promise," I replied. I leaned over and kissed his forehead and he reached his arms around my neck and gave me a hug only a child knows how to give. I couldn't ask for more.

As he laid his head back on his pillow, he explained, "Dogs really do go to Heaven, Dad. Someday Bella will die. I know that. When she does I will miss her but I know I will see her again in Heaven just like I'll see Grandpa. God loves dogs just like we do. Goodnight, Dad."

"Goodnight," I said as I closed the door to his bedroom, and inhaled the strength of his wisdom. I stood outside his door absorbing his words when other words he had spoken a few years ago found their way back into my memory. We were sitting together on the sofa and I had asked him what he wanted to be when he grew up.

He answered quite seriously, "I don't want to grow up. I like the little-kid costume I'm wearing."

His answer had surprised and amused me. I continued, "Do you really want to stay a little kid all of your life, or do you want to grow up someday like Dad.

His answer was simple. "When I am ready to grow up, I will just change my costume. But, today I will just keep the costume I have."

Today, he had changed his costume to one that fit him a little better but he is still wearing the costume of a child and I am grateful.

We had each played a role today. Walker and Will played the roles of brave little boys. Joanna and I had played the roles of, I think, competent parents and adults. We had handled the crisis well and everything turned out fine. We had remained calm in the face of panic.

I realized the adrenalin had stopped pumping and I was beginning to feel the fatigue that took its place. Warren and Weston waved goodnight as they headed for their bedroom and Joanna was sitting on the couch looking as tired as I felt.

"Do you think we performed well today, under the circumstances?" I asked.

"Do you mean did we perform well in not showing our panic or did we perform well in handling the situation?" She asked as she looked over at the sleeping animal on the pillow.

"Both," I answered. Just now realizing she had showed more bravery than she felt.

"To panic," she sighed, "I hope so. To the situation, I hope we never have to go through it again. I've been sitting here thinking, how do we train her," she motioned to the dog, " not to chase the fawns?"

"We'll have to find a way." I sounded more confident than I felt. "I thought we wore our costumes very well, though."

"What?" she asked, looking at me as if I had become delirious with fatigue.

"I was just remembering something Will told me a few years ago. He said that when he decided to grow up he would just change his costume," I laughed as I related the story. "There are times when I am in awe of the simple wisdom displayed by children.

"Today, you and I learned so much about our sons and from our sons as we experienced a moment in life with them." I found my way to the couch beside Joanna as I spoke.

"I was thinking that same thing as we were driving home," she said softly as she snuggled her head against my chest. "As we sat in the clinic and listened to Will sooth Walker's fears my fears were also soothed and I knew because Will knew that Bella would be fine.

Now, I think I'll trade in my costume of bravery for my sleep costume," she yawned and made her way to the bedroom.

I hadn't thought about life in the way Will had described it, but in a way we do all wear costumes of that which we think we are and who we want others to think we are. Some wear the costume of the victim while others wear the *success* costume. A person may wear the *always- broke* or *lonely* costume. Another person wears the *poor me* costume while another may wear a *I'll never be anything* costume. They then, take on the role that reflects the costume and find it difficult to experience who they really are, moment to moment, without the costumes.

I tore a piece of paper from the note pad on the table and jotted down this theory for future reference, then, as I reached down to turn out the lamp I felt as if there was something I had forgotten. It came to me that I needed to record the incredible events of this day in my journal.

Since my journal was not handy at the moment, I reached for my laptop that just happened to be sitting next to the lamp, on the table and punched the 'on' button. The room was illuminated by the screen as it came alive and I began to write. I wrote about Walker throwing the stick for Bella to chase. I wrote about the open house and how I felt as I read the things Will and Walker had written. I wrote, with a great deal of emotion, of the event that strengthened our lives as a family. Then I pushed 'save' on the laptop, turned it off and closed the lid.

As I checked Bella one more time to make sure she was comfortable I found another small body next to hers. Walker had slipped in while I was at the computer and made himself a bed next to the dog.

As I bent down to cover him he opened one little eye and in a sleepy voice whispered, "I didn't want Bella to be alone if she woke up in the night."

I smiled as I tucked his arm under the blanket, then I stood for a moment watching a little boy and a golden retriever sleep before turning out the light.

As I made my way to the bedroom in the dark, I realized I still hadn't discussed Peru with Joanna, but it could wait until tomorrow.

It has been two weeks since Bella had her incident. The bandage was gone now and the hair was beginning to cover the scars as it grew back and she's looking like her old self again, at least on the outside. On the inside there has been a change in her. Fear has found its way into her world confining her to a self-imposed prison. Even the offer of her favorite snack wouldn't bring her past a ten-foot radius surrounding the trailer.

Dogs aren't that much different than people when it comes to learning fear, I've decided. But, how do you talk to a dog about letting go of fear? I felt, for the first time in years, I was without an answer.

"Come on Bella," I said, scratching her behind the ear. "Let's go for a run. You'd like that, wouldn't you girl?"

She gazed up at me with sad, empty eyes. While the scars on the outside were fading, the scars on the inside were rooting themselves deep into her heart. Her tongue licked my arm without enthusiasm then she lay back down on her paws.

I sat in the chair next to her watching her while Weston coaxed her with a fresh bone from the dinner table. Nothing worked. The silence of her bark was almost deafening.

Fear is a strange phenomena. Something happens to us and we become intimately acquainted with it. Fear makes itself right at home in our hearts. It's our guest and we honor it and become comfortable with it and strangely enough are afraid to let it go.

"I wonder if she is afraid to go back to being the dog she was before, fearing she will get hurt again," Weston said as he tossed the bone to her. "It's an instinct, isn't it Dad, I mean not to want to get hurt?"

I looked at Bella and I suddenly missed the dog she had been just a few short weeks ago. I have helped hundreds of people let go of fear, but nothing in all my experiences had prepared me for this. I have no idea how to communicate those same ideas to a dog. How do I release her from her nightmare?

"What is opposite of fear, Dad? Isn't it courage and trust? Can we communicate trust through love? Will that be enough for now?" Weston asked, keeping his emotions in check. "Dogs understand love and they understand faith, right? Once she knows because we love her, she can trust us, maybe that will give her the courage she needs to not be afraid anymore."

"It's certainly worth a try," I answered.

"I'll get Will and Walker to help," Weston spoke with enthusiasm now, " and we'll each take a certain time every day playing with her and with each watch, we'll call it, we'll sit further and further away from the trailer when we call her to come until one day, without realizing it, she will have broken the invisible chain of fear. I think that will work, don't you, Dad? I'll bet Warren will even help between ball practices."

Bella lifted her head in response to the enthusiasm in Weston's voice. She gave a little bark and few whimpers then settled her head back onto her paws. I wondered if she understood what we were planning for her.

Weston grabbed the bone again and sat next to her. He began to stroke her fur and talk about the trees and the grass and what he had done yesterday. The dog responded with a whimper now and then but mostly listened quietly with her head on his lap, her eyes blinking.

I took Bella's dish and filled it with water, the heat had already made itself known and it was early yet. As I set the dish in front of the dog, she raised up, took a few laps of water, whimpered what I considered to be a 'thank you' then nuzzled her nose against Weston's leg, lifted one paw and extended it over his thigh.

This is unreal, I thought to myself as I focused on the scene in front of me. Do we have a case of self-pity here? Is it possible? She was exhibiting all the symptoms and I felt I was becoming the student once again. This time my teacher is a dog.

"Weston," I said, "you might need to be aware of something. I think her fear has developed into self-pity."

"I think I already knew that," he said softly, "but, I'm not sure what to do about it. I read in a book once that a dog responds to the tone of your voice as much as what you say. I think if we use a soft tone when we pet her and then work our way up to the command tone when we are coaxing her to come away from the trailer it might work."

"It just might," I agreed. "You could keep a chart for a few days on her responses and see if there is any progress. It might be a good idea for the three of you to leave her alone by the trailer at times, staying just close enough for her to see and hear you having fun. Your laughter might be her healer."

"Man, I almost forgot, Weston said as he moved his leg out from underneath Bella and stood up. "I've got to do a paper about energy for class on Tuesday. I need you to give me your theory on how energy affects us and the elements around us every day."

Today is Saturday, I'm on a break from work and my son wants me to discuss one of my favorite subjects. Couldn't have happened at a better time.

"Let's give Bella her alone time and we'll take a walk and talk about energy," the excitement must have unveiled itself in my voice because Weston gave me one of his all-knowing crooked grins.

"Look all around you, Weston," I began, "what do you see?"

"I see the grass and the trees, a few animals hunting for food. I see a house, half finished, and I see you, almost finished," he snickered. "A few more touches here and there and you'll look pretty good."

I laughed with him as I pulled his ball cap down to his nose. He had my eyes and his mother's hair, but his sense of humor was his own. I liked the combination.

"Everything you see is made up of energy; the tree, the grass, the animals, the house and even you and me are made up of energy.

"You mean my skin is made up of energy?" Weston asked, "and my hair? Everything inside of me is made of energy? That's cool."

I explained to him just as I explained to the people in my seminar a month ago that we arrive here on earth with a certain amount of energy and we can burn up the energy however we decide.

There is one universal law that is in effect at all times but there are two parts to the law. One is what I call the law of expansion and the other, the law of restriction, so the universe is expanding all the time which means this energy we are a part of is expanding all the time. We are a part of the universe so we should always be expanding and growing as well. We are in partnership with this energy and we can create anything we want."

The sun had found us among the oak trees and we began to search for seclusion from its rays.

" Do you know," I asked as we walked toward the huge Oak tree, "that we are the only species on the earth that have an imagination? A bear doesn't have one. A duck doesn't have one. These animals running around searching for food don't have one, and dogs don't have one. The all have instinct. How do you think ducks know to fly south in the winter?"

"By instinct. I read when it starts to get cold, instinct tells them to fly South." Weston replied as we sought a cool, shady spot under the same old Oak we had hugged not too long ago. A slight breeze drifted over us bringing with it the fragrance of our little forest.

"So this Oak tree is energy too, right Dad?" Kind of hard to believe something so big is made of pure energy, isn't it?"

"Not only is the tree you see made of energy but everything is about energy, even the energy we create inside of ourselves. Every thought that we think, every feeling we feel, every emotion we experience and every belief that we act out influences how we create, using energy.

We can use our imagination to expand or to restrict. Whether we are allowing ourselves to expand and be open for self-love and the good things in life, or restrict it with self-doubt, the law is always in place. We create what we feel. The law of restriction is where we take our imagination and create something and restrict that energy into a form. A physical form could be something like an automobile or an airplane or it could even be something like anger, fear or worry. It is a restricting of energy into physical form.

When you look at the word, e-motion – energy-in-motion. That's exactly what it is. Energy that we have inside of us is a trapped feeling when we experience an emotion, such as anger, it is the feeling that is trapped inside being put into motion. When it is in motion, I think it's God's way of telling us, "It's time to let go and release that energy."

"Why does it go into motion?" Weston asked as he picked up a handful of dead leaves and tossed them into the air, watching them as they fluttered to the ground.

"Just like those leaves are trapped by the breeze as they are tossed into the air, feelings get trapped inside of us when we have an experience," I explained. "When we think about something or see something that reminds us of the experience, the trapped energy of the feeling goes into motion giving us the opportunity to deal with it, or let it go if we choose."

"So when we feel sad and keep that feeling trapped inside, we are restricting energy. Is that right?" Weston's question reflected his understanding.

"Exactly. Let's call it *nobody loves me* energy. If a person had been hurt by someone in the past, they trap the feeling inside and it stays there until they decide to let it go and move on. This *nobody loves me* energy trapped inside you is as solid as a tree. The only difference is we call one a tree and other, *nobody loves me*. Just as God's imagination created a tree, someone's imagination created *nobody loves me*. Do you see any difference? It's really the same, only in a different form. And it stays in that form until it is released back into expanding, usable energy once again. In the case of the oak tree, if you cut a branch off and put it in a fire it burns up. It is no longer wood, but ahs been transformed back into energy."

"Then," Weston interrupted, "from the feeling we develop our beliefs, and from our beliefs, our behavior is derived, then we produce the result of our lives. If we feel less loving toward ourselves, we will experience that others feel less than loving toward us. Is that what you mean?"

I nodded, knowing he had nailed the concept.

"So," he continued, "if I am pitching in tomorrow's game and I walk someone and it makes me angry or frustrated with myself, until I deal with it and let it go, I have trapped the energy inside causing me to create more of the same? Is that what the coach means when he says, 'shake it off', after I throw a bad pitch?"

"Perfect example," I exclaimed. "We, in a way, write the story of our lives by our experiences and how we deal with those experiences. Everyone has a story. Some peoples story is, *never enough,* or *I will never make the money I need,* or *I'll never be a great pitcher because.* Or *I will never do enough with my life.* How we feel about ourselves is the story we'll create and live."

"Can we change our story? He asked.

"All we have to do is use our imagination and we can change our story. Remember that feeling energy that we have trapped inside? We have to bring the emotion of the trapped feelings energy to the surface so it can move out. Only then do we have the capacity to create a new story. You can't have the old story and the new story at the same time. What we are creating in our lives is based on experiences we've had, the behaviors we are acting out that are all based on experiences, feelings and beliefs. Only when you start to move that energy out, are you open for the beliefs to change.

What we experience as our story is all based on what we believe to be true. However, all beliefs are false."

Weston chimed in, "what do you mean all beliefs are false? If I believe something doesn't that make it true?"

"Well, yes and no. A belief is something that you have decided is true, but then it is only true for you. In other words, if you believe that you are not a good pitcher, that will be true for you, but it doesn't make it true for everyone. And the good news is that you can change that belief anytime you choose."

"So" Weston asked, "when Walker climbed the rope to the top and rung the bell he had to believe he could do it first, right?"

"That is correct. And once he did it the first time it just became second nature to him."

"Wow, that's heavy stuff. Thanks Dad, you've given me a lot of material to work with, and something to believe when I pitch tomorrow's game." Weston yawned as his eyelids fell. "Why is being here among the trees so relaxing?"

"It's because trees only operate in the present, while humans are most always mentally off somewhere else, but that's another story." I replied as my lids slipped peacefully over my eyes. "Remind me to tell you my theory on living in the present, some day."

Reflections

Journal entry

In my child's eyes the words were spoken.
In his hug, the truth whispered through.
Words not voiced, yet never to be forgotten
I'm here to teach you that I love you.

He giggled as he hugged me tighter,
I laughed and hugged him tighter too.
As I felt the words reveal their meaning,
I'm here to teach you that I love you.

My thoughts jump back and forth as I write, and my chest tightens as I think about a little boy, with his arms around my neck, and I hear the words, "I'm here to teach you that I love you." Then, I smile to myself as a picture of Walker comes into my mind, climbing the rope and ringing the bell and I am reminded of a discovery I made some time ago. Resourceful energy can be used to overcome all obstacles. When we align ourselves with the source we will achieve unparalleled success and happiness.

When the mind is mature enough to receive.
The miracle of what it can achieve
Then the world is at your feet.

When the spiritual faith of a child brings the power of healing,
To quiet the fears, and sooth the emotion of feeling.
Then earth and heaven meet.

Stepping inside a child's classroom is like stepping inside a child's mind,
You observe, then you marvel at the things you find.
For it's a child's world you've entered.

Stepping inside a child's world is like stepping inside a child's heart
Once you find the way there, it's very hard to part,
With the memories you have stirred.

There is one memory, at first, I would have erased from the hearts of my sons. The day the doe attacked Bella. Yet, in retrospect, that experience expanded our insight and penetrated our hearts with love and compassion, not only for Bella, but for each other. Would I be wise to protect my sons from all unpleasant things?

>*If I protect them from sorrow,*
>*And the pain it brings.*
>*I undermine their compassion,*
>*And stifle their empathy.*
>
>*If I protect them from all danger*
>*That walks along their path*
>*I will take from them, strength*
>*And cripple their insight.*
>
>*If I protect them from life,*
>*And it's experiences.*
>*I rob them of wisdom,*
>*And weaken their character*
>
>*If I take away their trials*
>*And do not let them stumble*
>*I suppress their learning,*
>*And limit their knowledge.*

All these things they must experience
And understand for themselves
Only then can they realize
The depth of their soul.

Sometimes it is so difficult to wear the costume of an adult and to do all the adult things that must be done. How does a parent know when to protect and when to step back and allow the child to be on his own?

I'm not sure you can have that same philosophy, however, with a dog. Sometimes you just have to protect dogs.

Thought for today

I love, love, more than anything
But when I feel God's love,
His love is the love I love the best
…Will

Chapter Seven

Two days have passed since we napped under the oak tree. I looked in the mirror at my sunburn. It could have been worse. Both sides of my face could have been exposed.

"Hey, Dad," Weston called as he came toward the bathroom. "I finished my paper on energy and I'd like you to read it. The teacher gave us the choice. We could either write a report or a story. I decided a story would be more fun." He laughed as he looked at my face. "It could have been worse, both sides could have been kissed by the sun, as mom would say. Here I'll leave this with you." He handed me a folder. "Could you read it today, I have to hand it in tomorrow. By the way, we started working with Bella and I'm keeping a chart on her progress. She has expanded her territory by five feet, so maybe by the weekend we'll have her running and jumping again. Oh, and Mom said she would pick up your shirts on her way back from taking us to school."

"One question before you leave. Where's your sunburn?"

He smiled as he gave me a sympathetic look. "Mom won't let us out of the house without being plastered with the strongest sunscreen she can find." With that bit of information he was gone.

How could spring allow the sun to be this cruel, I thought as I looked into the mirror. While I had napped it slowly crept from behind the tree and, with its brush, painted the left side of my face a subtle shade of red. I suppose I should be grateful that it wasn't any worse. I didn't mention it to

Weston, but I don't believe in using sunscreen. I think exposure to the sun in small doses triggers your body to produce what it needs to protect you from the sun's harmful rays. That's why there is a higher incidence of skin cancer in the areas of the country where you get very little sun. People in those areas get too much too fast.

I glanced at the folder in my hand, then back at my sorrowful reflection. Which one needed the most attention? It was a toss-up so I ran the comb through my hair, rubbed some aloe on the sunburn, then found a comfortable spot on the couch and opened the folder to read Weston's story.

Energy in Action

By Weston Britt

All through the universe, colonies of cosmic energy exist. Without them there would be only emptiness. With them there are planets, stars, and atmosphere. There are animals, trees and plants. But most important of all, there are human beings.

When these particles of energy are combined, they create intelligence. The question is; could one particle, all by itself, think and be an energy being, and could each tiny energy being have a personality all its own?

Why not! Maybe, they have their own little planet where they live in colonies, and have families and friends, and all the little children particles of energy go to school to prepare for their futures just like we do.

This is the story of particle beings called Ergs who live in the colony of Ergon. Population: three-hundred billion. I'll not describe their physical appearance, but will leave that to the imagination of the reader.

The story begins as Baryon, a very intelligent particle of energy, is meeting his friends one morning, in front of their school.

Muon, who is very fearless and besides that, likes to have lots of fun, is Baryon's best friend. The quark triplets, Q, Ua and R.K., who are never separated, (and talking to one is like talking to all three because they all three listen to what you say, and answer as if they have just one voice), are his next best friends. Kaon, who is very shy and studies a lot, and rides a mean space-board, and has pretty dark green hair, is kind of like his girlfriend.

I heard a truck pull into the driveway. I looked out the window just in time to see three more trucks carrying building supplies coming up the road. Construction was about to begin on the house once again. Joanna would be thrilled when she got home. I set Weston's paper down long enough to answer the doorbell, and the broad smile of the foreman greeted me as I opened the door.

"Thought you might like to know that we have approval to complete the house as long as there are no more changes," he laughed. "Tell your wife we'll be working six days a week so we can get it finished for her." With that he turned and waved his hand, climbed in his truck and was on his way to the house. He was, I decided a man of action, and few words.

I watched, through the window for a several minutes, as the men began unloading the supplies, before going back to the couch and Weston's story.

It was the beginning of the second rotation of classes. The six friends had decided to meet in front of the complex where their classes were held. Baryon was the first to arrive. While he waited he tapped his CCD (Charge-Coupled Device) to review his classes. His first class lit up in green, Advanced Energy Composition of the Human Species. That would be his toughest class, he knew, because the human species was the most complex of all energy make-ups.

He touched the CCD again and the screen glowed in orange, Problem Solving of Energy in Numbers. Each time he touched the screen a different color would appear as the class was illuminated - Where We Come From, in blue, Space Time and How to

Tell, in purple. Lit in red was, *Understanding the Big Bang*, one of the elective classes offered.

"Hi, anti-gravity travel is moving pretty slow this morning," said Muon as he came to a stop. "Let's see if we have any classes together." He quickly lit up his CCD and where Baryon's light had been green, Muon's showed a yellow glow displaying, Mass, Charge and Spin. The rest of the classes were the same.

Before they could celebrate their luck, however, Kaon came floating by on her space-board. "Hi guys," she shouted, as she made a loop before coming to a stop. "I've got "Making Flower Fragrances 105, first. I don't suppose either one of you are taking that class?"

Both Baryon and Muon shook their heads.

"I'll take that as a definite NO," she giggled.

Finally the *Quark* triplets arrived, late as usual. "Sorry we're late," they chimed in unison, "but we couldn't find our book on *Rules of Quantum Mechanics*, and that's our first class, after *Nutrition and Ergs*, of course."

As *Nutrition and Ergs* was a required class and was given first thing each morning, and not a popular class to anyone, the friends slowly made their way to room $[x/y=2]$ and Professor Fermion, whose prime objective was to take care of every one of the 1.2 billion students.

"What did you choose as your elective?" Kaon asked the triplets as they made their way to Professor Fermion's room.

"The E's of Trees, what is yours?" they responded.

"Anti-matter and Energy," Kaon answered. "I'm taking it just for fun though. I'm hoping that when we get our assignments for our futures I get assigned to a flower."

"That's still a whole minuscule fraction of a second away," said Baryon as they sat in their seats.

"I know," Kaon said, "but I can hardly wait."

The rotation went quickly just as Kaon hoped it would. They had field trips to view the Twister and Quantum theories, and they viewed the energetic subatomic collisions that naturally occur throughout the atmosphere because of cosmic rays.

Finally, the time came when they were to receive their assignments. Before their graduation, however, the professors had planned a spectacular finale. All 1.2 billion students sat together and witnessed the Super Proton Synchrotron (SPS). It was the highlight of competition where a beam of protons was directed against an opposing beam of antiprotons. The clash liberated 540 billion electron volts of energy. It was incredible. It received a standing ovation. It was the perfect ending to their graduation.

The assignments were, then, handed out in sealed envelopes. After the ceremony, Baryon, Muon, Kaon and the triplets quickly found each other because they had promised they would open them together.

"You're first, Kaon," the triplets voices echoed each other, they were so excited.

Kaon opened her letter, glanced at it, then a smile the size of a proton crossed her face. "I've been assigned flowers," she shouted gleefully. "Not only that, but my specialty will be fragrance." Everyone applauded as she put the paper to her lips and gave it a big kiss.

"What else does it say?" prompted Muon, wanting to move on.

"It says, that I'm going to a place called Hawaii where flowers are always in bloom and will be a part of many fragrances before I return."

"That's cool," Baryon laughed. "You'll be a celebrity."

Next it was the Quark triplets turn and although they had the same assignment they each had a letter to open, which they did in synchronization. Their eyes moved as if connected to the same muscle and their mouths as if they were on the same hinge. "We are going to be a tree... we are going to be a tree...we are going to be a tree," their eyes lit up like the Milky Way as they continued reading, "You will be assigned to the Redwood Forest." They stopped and looked at each other, then started jumping and hugging each other as they shouted, "The Redwood Forest...the Redwood Forest...The Redwood Forest." The other three joined in, then Kaon suddenly stopped.

"But that means you could be gone for hundreds of years, earth time," she murmured, "cause trees are always happy and live in the moment."

Quiet settled over the group as they looked at her. None of them had realized, until this very moment, that they would no longer be together every day. These assignments would take them far away from each other for a very long time, maybe forever. Tears began to form in six pair of eyes as they hugged each other. "Wait, before we get too carried away here, let's see where Baryon and I are going." announced Muon as he held out his letter.

"Open it, hurry," Kaon said as she wiped the tears from her eyes.

Muon quickly broke the seal on the letter and unfolded it. He read it as his friends waited impatiently. "I am assigned to a lion in Africa," he smiled, pride showing on his face.

Ooooh's were heard all around him. "That's a powerful assignment," the triplets whispered. "But you are strong, and never afraid. We are so proud of you."

Everyone applauded and cheered then turned their eyes to Baryon. The seal holding his letter shut was still unbroken and his heart was beating so loudly, it was thudding in his ears.

"It's your turn," Muon said, giving him a poke.

Baryon's hands were shaking as he tore the seal. Inside was his fate and he almost didn't want to know for fear his assignment was going to be a bird or a fish. Slowly he opened the letter and lowered his eyes to read, You have been given the most arduous assignment of all. You will be required to show great courage and patience. You are assigned a human being. The duration of your assignment is unknown, but you have been given a human being of great character and strength, yet with many needs. As you know through your studies, you will be required to use your full strength at all times for a human being is the only species who can create and who has an imagination that use up a lot of energy. As you are aware, their emotions use tremendous amounts of energy, so it is possible that all you are made up of will be depleted causing a full burn out before the human has completed his life span, in which you will no longer be...

"We are waiting," chorused Baryon's friends.

Baryon didn't need to read any further. He knew it was the most dangerous assignment but he had wanted it anyway because it would also be the most exciting. He looked at his friends standing there, anticipation written all over their faces and he handed his letter to Muon who almost grabbed it out of his hand.

"He's assigned a human being," Muon's voice was almost reverent.

There was complete silence, all eyes on Baryon. Then, one by one, by three, they gave him a hug.

"Where are you going?" asked Kaon quietly

"It says here," answered Muon before Baryon could speak, "that he will be going to Oklahoma."

"The human being that gets you will be so powerful, Baryon," R.K said softly.

"So powerful!" echoed Q and Ua.

The six friends made a circle, their arms wrapped around each other and, knowing they might never see Baryon again, still they vowed they would meet in another time and space.

THE END

Stuck to the back of the last page was a large stick-um note in Weston's handwriting: *Dad, Maybe the story is fiction, then again, maybe it's not, who knows! Maybe Baryon was assigned to Jim from Oklahoma. If so, you better do things right. You wouldn't want a little particle of energy to miss out on a reunion with his friends because of you.*

P.S. The names of the characters in my story are actual names of space particles.

Thought you might want to know that.

Weston had taken my theory of energy and entwined it with imagination as well as fact and, in doing so, had written a story that not only gave insight to cosmetic energy, but was intriguing to read as well.

I heard Joanna's car pull into the driveway and waited for her to come into the trailer. I wanted her to read this story. After waiting several minutes, however, I decided she had bypassed the trailer for a more important quest. I looked out the window toward the house and found her standing in front of it, her back toward me and her right hand shading her eyes from the sun as she talked with the foreman. With her left hand she was pointing toward the covered porch area of the house and I found myself secretly praying that she wasn't making another change.

I slipped Weston's story back into the folder and set it on the table and, with some trepidation, made my way down the stairs of the trailer and toward the house. I hadn't walked twenty yards when I heard Bella whimpering, and as I turned around to her, I could see the sadness in her eyes. I coaxed her to come but she would only prance back and forth behind her invisible barrier. I didn't want to leave her and I could see she wasn't coming with me so I walked back and as I sat on the step, Bella laid down beside me her paws under her chin. I leaned over and stroked her coat and she moved a little closer until she was almost on my lap.

I had an idea. "Bella," I said, "let me tell you a story about energy."

She listened quietly as I retold the story, only I replaced the lion with a dog named Bella. That seemed to perk her up a little. As I was finishing the story, I stood and began to walk. She immediately got to her feet and followed. I knew I had to keep talking to keep her attention on me.

"See, Bella, they are working on the house again." I motioned as we walked a little further. "I think I will like this new home, what do you think, girl?"

Bella's reply was a soft bark, as she stayed close beside me. The important thing was that she was staying with me. I hadn't realized I could feel such compassion for an animal, but I suppose compassion knows no boundaries. The feeling of true compassion is so strong and has such profound quality that it extends the barriers. I guess I would define genuine compassion as a feeling of unbearableness at the sight of another's suffering whether it is a person or an animal. The more one understands the various kinds of suffering, the deeper the level of one's compassion, and a deep feeling of connection is formed. I could feel the connection and the need to reach out to Bella and let her know that I understood.

"Since I have your undivided attention, Bella, I want to tell you something I haven't told anyone else in the family. I'm thinking of taking a trip to Peru in the fall, what do you think about that?"

From the corner of my eye I could see her hesitate. It could be that she didn't like the idea of me going to Peru, but I'll assume we had just passed her safety zone. I continued to walk slowly. She whimpered but she followed.

"I want to tell you another story. This one is about a policeman from San Francisco who attended my seminar several months ago. Have you got a few minutes?"

Bella looked up at me, a soft, melancholy growl escaped from deep inside her. I think she was either begging me to stop walking or keep talking. I chose to believe she wanted to hear the story so I continued.

"This policeman had been on a sabbatical leave from the force for twelve years. He was seeing a psychiatrist three times a week.

The reason he couldn't work was that he had been involved in a shootout twelve years before. A couple of people were killed including a small boy and he, himself had been wounded. When he came to, this little boy was laying on top of him, dead. He didn't know if he had shot him or what had happened because it was all a blur in his mind. He couldn't get rid of all that was going on inside of him until he came to the class.

He said to me, 'I have gone to therapists for twelve years. Not one of them told me that I could let it go. We would analyze it, we talked about it and we walked through it and by the time I'd get to the elevator it would be right back again. I now know what to do. I knew I had it in me but I didn't know how or why I had it in me. My only explanation to myself was that it was an experience and memory.'

Once he experienced it, he started moving the trapped energy of the experience and then he let it go. He was back to work in thirty days. You see, Bella, he was his own judge and jury and he had sentenced himself. Yet he was able to let go once he eliminated self-judgement."

We had walked about twenty more feet by the time I had finished the story and we were well beyond the invisible line she refused to cross three days earlier, but now Bella would go no further. We were getting to close to the place where she had been attacked.

"In a way, Bella, you have sentenced yourself." I knelt down, put a hand on each side of her face and looked into her sad eyes. "I wish I knew how to help you let the fear go. It's ok, girl, don't worry, we'll find a way."

Bella licked my hand with a wet doggy kiss, which, usually, I'm not particularly fond of, but this time I didn't mind. I gave her a scratch behind the ear, then stood and started back toward the trailer with the family dog at my heels.

Joanna spotted us and called for us to wait. When she reached us she was smiling the same smile that I imagined Keon had smiled when she found out she was assigned the fragrance of flowers.

"Guess what? They think they can have the house done before summer brings the real heat," she laughed as she looked at my sunburn. "Could have been worse."

"So I've been told," I whined, sounding almost as sorrowful as Bella.

"I see Bella has ventured out a little farther, today. How did you get her to leave the trailer?"

"I told her stories,"

"You what?"

"I told her stories," I repeated. "But once we got close to the house, she refused to go any farther. Even my stories couldn't entice her."

We left Bella at the door and went into the trailer where I handed Joanna the folder containing the story Weston had written and explained how it came about. "Give me your opinion when you have finished reading it. I'll be in my office." Office being a makeshift room which will eventually be a garage once the house is finished. In desperate situations, you do desperate things. The trailer just was not big enough for my 4'x6' cluttered desk.

The phone was ringing when I opened the door to my office. It was Steve, the producer for my infomercials.

"I wanted to run some ideas by you before I went any further with this idea I had," he said. We spent the next ten minutes tossing ideas back and forth, before coming to a conclusion.

"Now to change the subject," I chuckled, "I've been invited to do a spiritual retreat in Peru. I'd like your opinion."

"My opinion is," Steve responded with the same chuckle. "They could put you in an airplane, and then drop you out of the plane, with a parachute, over any city, with empty pockets, and you would create what you would need. You're at home anywhere. Pretty soon you would meet someone and get to know them and, within a short time, you would be starting a business. I think that's why I like working with you."

After hanging up the phone I realized what Steve had said was true. When I decide to do something, I just go do it. I say "Yes" and then figure out how. Sometimes it takes me longer to decide, but once I make the decision it becomes part of my agenda. Everything in its time. Life is a journey, just open the door and there it is. We make it what it is, I choose life to be an adventure as well as a journey, and so it is.

Someone asked me once if I write down my goals? The answer was no. I don't think I have any goals I just decide I want to do something then I do it. Most of the time I don't even think of it as a goal and I sure don't have to write it down to remember it. I figure that if you've made a firm decision, you should be able to remember it without writing it down.

Once you're clear about your vision, it's just as important to let go of your vision as it is to let go of your fears. It's not our job to force things to happen in our lives. It's our job to create the clear vision. It's like taking a camera, we see the picture, frame it, focus, then snap it. When we have fear, we see the 'perfect picture', focus it, frame it, snap it, then we open up the camera to see if it worked. When we cling to our vision we are also clinging to the fear of it not happening. So my philosophy is to make the decision, create the vision in your imagination of your desired outcome, let go of the need to control the outcome, then take action toward what you want.

If there is something you would love to have in your life, and once the decision is made, you focus, then frame it. You must ask yourself why, to gain greater clarity as to the real reason, or the essence of why you want it. You say; yes, this is what I want, this is how I want to feel. Snap. At that point you have to let go of everything that doesn't move you toward that vision, knowing that what you feel inside is what you will create. I call this, self-observation. When you feel something, you connect your head with your heart. Create your vision, then let go of the need to control the outcome. Find your fear, if you have one, then let go of it. I wonder how I explain that to a dog.

I had a dream several years ago. In this dream I was standing in a room. To the right of me twelve men in black robes sat on twelve white chairs. In the center was a large desk. A man wearing a black judges robe, with a gavel in his hand, sat behind the desk. To my left, stood my friend, Michael. He was dressed in an exquisite white robe and I knew, without a doubt, he was an angel.

Michael was trying to tell me something, but I couldn't make out his words, yet the room was still except for the sound of his voice. When he realized that I couldn't understand him, he closed his mouth, and with his hand, he motioned for me to come closer, then he took my arm and led me to the twelve men sitting on the white chairs.

"What do you see?" he asked me. And though he spoke as a whisper, this time his words filled my head.

As I looked at each man, it was as if I was looking into a mirror. I turned to Michael, "I don't understand, what does this mean?"

Michael was silent, but directed my attention to the man with the gavel. The man raised his head and as he did, I saw myself again. "Help me to understand," I begged him.

"You had a question in your heart that needed my attention," he answered. What is that question, Jim?"

"I'm not sure what you mean."

"Think. Remember in your heart you have asked who would have the right to judge you, in the end. Look around you, Jim, what do you see? Tell me what you see."

"I see what appears to be a court room with twelve jurors. I see a judge sitting on the bench. They all could be me, Michael," I spoke as my voice echoed in the stillness of the room.

"They are you, Jim. This is the answer to your question. No one will judge you more harshly than you will judge yourself. You will be your own judge and jury. There will be many who will stand beside you, like I am now, with nothing but love for you. Only you will stand against you. Do you understand now?"

The dream had faded then but it left me with a knowledge that God doesn't judge us, how can he? God is pure love and love does not judge. We judge ourselves.

I gathered the notes I had made the night before and spread them over the desk and read through each one. I picked up the last one I had been working on and read the words aloud. *We have been told somewhere along the line by someone we love and respect, that there is something wrong with us, and at some point we begin to believe them and we decide, that is who we really are. At that point the judge is born. This internal judge starts weighing out what is right or wrong, good or bad, based on how we feel about ourselves. Our internal defense attorney then tells us what we have to do in order to receive the attention we want, the attention that validates who we want to be. We, then, become pulled in two different directions, who we really are deep inside, and who we've come to believe we are based upon our experiences and what we've been told. It's like driving our car with one foot on the brakes and the other on the gas, and wondering why we're not getting where we want to go. When we grow up and become adults we continue to act these things out in our lives, searching for self-love and happiness, and at the same time, beating ourselves up for not being good enough or deserving happiness. It shows in our relationships, careers, family, health, etc.*

I wanted to add that no one intentionally sets up the plan for it to happen. No parent deliberately says, *I'm going* to *cause this*. No one is to blame. A belief is born and we start to judge ourselves. We say, *I am not good enough*, or *I can't forgive myself*. We get caught up in a never-ending, mutually supporting cycle. *I want more love in my life*, but our belief is, *I don't deserve it. I hate myself for feeling this way*, but our belief is, *I must feel this way in order to survive*. Our own self-judgement keeps us away from being happy. We, then, compare ourselves to others and grade ourselves accordingly.

Before I could finish my note, however, Joanna appeared with the pages of Weston's story in her hand.

"What did you think?" I asked

"I think he takes after his father." She hesitated as she set the story on my desk, "Will this be safe among the clutter or shall I take it back to the trailer?" Without waiting for an answer she retrieved the sheets of paper and continued, "Seriously, I will always remember the names of a few energy particles because I read this adorable story. I know more about cosmic energy than I did before and will probably remember it longer because I will relate it to the story. Oh, one more thing, I will be able to sleep better now that I know Baryon is part of your make-up." She stopped talking long enough to give me quick peck on the check. "Now I have to get back, I left Bella whimpering on your lounge chair, she doesn't seem to care for my stories."

Joanna took a small package of almonds out of her pocket and handed them to me as she turned to leave. "Warren picked these up at the convenience store when we stopped to get gas. He said your almond bowl was almost empty. My instructions were to fill the bowl for you, but Bella needs me more."

After she left I opened the package and emptied it into a small wooden bowl that had 'ALMUNDS' written on the side in a little boy's handwriting.

How many years has that little bowl set in my office? I remembered that I was about to leave on a three-day trip for a workshop I was presenting. I had taken some things to the car and noticed some almonds had just fallen from out of the tree we had so I found a small box to gather some to take with me.

Warren approached me, watched for a few minutes, then asked, "what'er you doin', Dad?"

I glanced up at him, "Gathering a few almonds," I said as I closed the lid on the box and set it in the car.

"While you're gone, what would you pay me to gather a box of almonds?"

"A couple of bucks," I replied.

When I returned, three days later, Warren met me at the car with a big smile. "You owe me thirty-six bucks," he said as he opened my door.

"For what?" I asked.

"For the eighteen boxes of almonds I gathered," he replied.

As I remembered, the deal was for one box, at least that's what I thought, but I didn't have the heart to tell him so I simply asked to see them. He led me to the garage where a huge pile of almonds was sitting in the middle of the floor.

"There are eighteen boxes there," he said. "I'll put them into boxes to show you, if you want."

"That won't be necessary, I believe you." I wondered how such a little guy picked all those almonds by himself, because most of them were still on the tree when I left, so I asked, "How did you gather so many in such a short period of time?"

"Well, Dad," he said as he folded his arm across his chest, "you know the game gear I bought, or rather, we bought?"

I nodded.

"Well, my friend down the street wanted to sell this game that worked in my player at a really good deal, so I told him if he would come and help me I would buy his game for twenty-six dollars."

"That's pretty creative," I admitted, feeling rather proud of him. "So the two of you filled the eighteen boxes?"

"Nope, not exactly, when he was helping me, he remembered that his brother owned half of the game and should be helping him pick, so he went home and got him. So we had three people picking almonds, but we were having a really hard time getting them out of the tree because they were up so high. You know Bill, our neighbor across the street?"

I nodded again, it was his story and I didn't want to interrupt.

"Well, Bill was walking by and I asked him if he liked almonds. He said, yes he did, very much. So I said, 'If you will get up in the trees and hit the limbs with a stick, I'll give you a box of almonds,' so he did. It only took us two hours. Could I have the thirty-six bucks now so I can go get the game?"

Talk about a win/win. This was a multiple win. The two brothers won by selling the game. Bill, the neighbor, won by getting the box of almonds that he loved. Warren won by getting the game he wanted, and ten dollars to boot. Even though I financed the whole business, I won by seeing my son use the power of his imagination to create a situation where everyone involved came out a winner. Besides, I really like almonds, especially fresh off the tree.

The almond bowl was a gift he bought with some of the extra money he had in his pocket after making his purchase. It was, he said, to stay in my office and always be full of almonds from our tree. Even though we moved a short time later and left that almond tree behind, the bowl has remained in my office, wherever it has been located, and is always filled with almonds, thanks to Warren.

I spent the next few hours working on the material for my Seminar in San Diego, then my stomach reminded me I hadn't eaten any breakfast, and it was almost time for lunch. Usually Often times Joanna brought lunch to me, if she was home, but the sun would be shining on the opposite side of my face if I walked to the trailer, and I needed to even the color up a little.

When Bella saw me, she started barking and came running toward me until she got to the spot where she stopped this morning. There she waited for me to come to her.

As I entered the trailer I had hoped I would find lunch waiting but, instead, the table was bare and Joanna was sitting in her chair staring at a photo in her hand. Silent tears made their way down her face. Without looking up she said simply, "My mother is dying."

I walked over and knelt down beside her. "I'm so sorry, Joanna," I said, gently taking her hand in mine.

She looked at me, her eyes red from crying. "My brother called and said they had taken her to the hospice house. There is nothing else they can do for her, Jim."

I reached over and pulled her close to me and held her while she wept openly. "I need to be with her through this," she spoke through the tears. "She has to see this picture of the oak tree so she will know where I'll be when I need to talk to her after she dies."

"I'll call the airlines and get you a ticket on the first available flight," I said, "while you pack." Lunch forgotten, I made reservations for Joanna on the noon flight the next day, then I went into the bedroom to help her pack.

REFLECTIONS

Journal entry

I have discovered the center of my universe. It lies in the learning. Today I learned that you can't trust the sun.

    A kiss from the sun. How do I return the favor?
    The sun is the giver
    And asks for nothing in return.
    I am an example of its humor.

There is so much to discover about the mind and it's possibilities. What is truth and what is fiction, I wonder!

    A story full of imagination. Is it fiction or is it truth?
    We only see our own dimension,
    We are our own restriction.
    How will we know?

    What would I discover if I were a tree,
    A lion or a flower?
    For a day or just an hour.
    Would my wisdom grow?

    Dog and man, though different, fear is the same?
    Will stories quiet the mind?
    Or is fear too confined?
    Walk with me, we'll find a way.

Life is a journey, everything in its time.
Open the door, walk through,
Life is what you choose.
Tomorrow and today.

We create our own success
No goal, just a vision
And then the decision
To do it, then let it go.

We see the perfect picture
We focus it, we frame it
Snap! Then we create it.
Live it, and it is so.

In my dream I look around me.
I see Michael standing there.
He whispers the secret we share
And I listen to my guide

In the courtroom of my mind there is no man to judge me
Only those who stand beside me,
With love alone to guide me.
It is I who will decide.

A little boy and an almond tree
The memory flows back to me
As I see the power of an imagination
Put to work through his creation,
This little boy so full of life.

I've learned today that I will never get tired of eating almonds as long as they are a gift from my son.

Thought for Today

If we focus on our inner harmony,
our personality will reflect a certain peace
that can only come from knowing our own inner spirit.

Chapter Eight

The house seemed strangely quiet when I returned from taking the boys to school. Joanna has been gone for almost three weeks now and I am just beginning to understand a mother's world.

Helping four boys get ready for charter school is an event within itself. But first comes breakfast. I am now converted to cold cereal or a bagel with cream cheese, juice on the side. With the six-year old, the conversation goes something like this;

"Dad, where's my green shirt?"

"Haven't seen it lately, did you look in the closet?"

"Mom always knows where my green shirt is."

"Good for her."

Another voice is heard, "Your shirt is where you left it day before yesterday, after you decided not to wear it to school."

Silence.

"Dad, I can't find my left shoe."

"Did you take if off with the right shoe?"

"Yeh, but it's not there anymore."

"Sorry to interrupt," Warren said as he walked into the kitchen. "But, if you have time today, Dad, could you do some laundry, we're running low on necessities."

"Didn't I just do laundry?"

"Ah...I think that was a week ago," he gave me a sympathetic smile. "Also, can you pick me up from school at 3:30, instead of 2:30?"

"Write it on the list for today so I'll remember," I sighed.

"Dad," Walker's voice was heard again. "Mom always knows where my shoes are. I'll be glad when she comes home."

"I'll go help Walker find his shoe while you finish making the lunches," Warren said as he moved toward the shared bedroom.

I think I will be happier than Walker when Joanna comes home. Taking the responsibility of both parents at once is much more difficult than I had anticipated. For example, I didn't know that if you put little sheets of fabric softener in the dryer, it eliminates static cling, or that Clorox doesn't whiten everything. I didn't know washing machines ate socks, and clothes hampers are always full no matter how often you empty them. I didn't know little boy's shoes could lose themselves, and that shirts love to play hide-n-seek.

I now know that towels are always in short supply and in great demand, that my cooking isn't that good and take-out isn't that bad, and that dishes multiply in the sink and subtract in the cupboard. I found that a vacuum refuses to pick up just anything lying around on the carpet, and complains with full intensity when expected to do so.

I realize that a mother's touch is impossible for a father to try to imitate, and that the house is cozier when she is home.

"I'm here now." Walker said as he appeared around the corner, fully dressed, and shoes on both feet. He took one look at the lunch sacks sitting on the cupboard and gave a mournful sigh.

"I see you found the other shoe," I commented. "Great detective work."

"Warren found it. When's Mom going to be home? I really do miss her and she makes really great lunches."

I smiled to myself, I guess my lunches haven't been getting good reviews either.

"Is Grandma going to die?" Walker's voice was quiet now as he handed me a comb.

"I think so, Walker." I said. I knelt down beside him and kissed his forehead before running the comb through his hair. This little boy's world has been turned upside down because his mother had not been here to help him find his shoes and to make his lunch, and to hug him when he gets home from school and before he goes to bed. His Grandmother is dying and he doesn't know what to do about any of it.

Yet as I combed his hair, I felt his eyes searching my face, then he placed his hands on my shoulders, and with concern in his voice he whispered, "I know you will be glad when Mom comes home, too, Dad. Don't worry, I will make sure both of my shoes are by my bed tonight, and you make pretty good lunches." Then he reached up and kissed my cheek before turning, retrieving his lunch sack and stuffing it into his backpack. "I'm ready now," he said as he led the rest of us out to the car.

Now, as I put things back in order, and the trailer echoes the noise of the dishes, the words Weston spoke that day as we sat discussing life in a trailer, began to focus in my mind. *It isn't anything in particular until we all step inside, then it becomes something beautiful because love has filled it with its radiance.* I smiled as I thought to myself, it's also filled with welcome noise and laughter, lost shoes and a temperamental vacuum, overflowing clothes hampers and...oops, I almost forgot. Quickly I sorted the clothes and started the washer. We hooked up the washer and dryer in an unfinished home. I had to lie to the inspector. I told him they were not operable I just had to store them there. He bought the story, or maybe he just felt sorry for us and let it pass. Either way, we had a washer and dryer. With that done, I had work waiting for me at my office that needed as much attention as the trailer did.

I had expected Bella to be waiting at the foot of the steps for me when I closed the door to the trailer, but she has found a new group of friends. It has taken two weeks of constant coaxing and working with her to get her to finally break through her fear, but it worked. At the beginning of the second week Will and Walker would go just beyond her safety zone and play catch, then one of them would toss the ball to her and coax her to bring it back. The first two days, she would drop the ball where she had created her invisible shield, and refused to take another step. On the third day, however, when Warren and Weston took their turn, she couldn't stand it any longer and crossed the self-imposed line and found that she was fine. Since that day, she has been reunited with freedom and reacquainted with the woods, and the squirrels, the rabbits and the birds, much to their dismay.

She has even made herself at home with the carpenters and the painters who are working on the house, and barks out her approval or disapproval of work done, with enthusiasm. The men share their lunches with her and converse with her as if she were one of them. Maybe it's just my imagination but I think the work is moving faster with her help. The foreman told me yesterday he would have us in the house in two weeks.

When Joanna calls today I'll have to share the good news with her. She could use some good news. In just a few short weeks she will finally have a home and space, I will have a home office, and we will be able to park the car where I now do business. The boys will each have their own bedroom, and Bella can come in and take a nap any time she pleases without someone stepping on her. Of course she will have to have house rules orientation first. Come to think of it, maybe we will all have to have house rules orientation, it's been almost seven months since we have actually lived in a house.

There were six men plus Bella working on the house this morning. The outside was all but finished in authentic Santa Fe Style architecture. It's a spacious home, spread over seventy-four hundred square feet. There's several covered porches where we will spend a great deal of our time during the summer months. There is a nice sized pool and Jacuzzi along with a fully equipped outdoor kitchen with a wood fired brick oven that can't wait to try out. It was simply beautiful to look at and I was pleased. I stopped and admired it wishing Joanna could be here to watch the progress with me.

I opened the door to my office, looked at the mail stacked on my desk and wondered where to begin. Luckily the ringing of the phone made the decision easier. As I said hello into the receiver, the voice on the other end quickly responded. "Oh, I'm so glad I caught you. Remember the woman you sat next to on your flight to New York City several weeks ago?"

I recognized the voice then, "Of course I do." I answered, "how are you doing?"

"Great, and it's all because of you. I want to apologize again for my rudeness in the beginning stages of our conversation. I wasted a lot of valuable time, while I was wallowing in self- pity and blame. I need to tell you that after we parted, I wrote down my new feelings on a piece of paper, then I wrote down the ways in which I had been trying to control my husband. I read them through twice to make sure I had them all, then I simply tore the paper into little shreds and threw them away. I had to make sure I was letting go, and do you know something, it worked. It really worked. It wasn't easy at first. It was like I was stepping onto the stage with the same cast, except for my lines, they had all been changed. Once I learned the new lines, however, the scene began to flow and I feel happier now than I have in years."

"And your husband, how is he doing?"

There was a soft laugh on the other end. "At first I think he was sure I had suffered a slight stroke, but then, as time went on, he began to respond to the change in me and I began to recognize the man I had married and the reason I had married him." There was silence on the other end for several seconds and I sensed her emotions.

"I would not be honest," she continued, the emotion showing itself in her voice, "if I didn't tell you I had to come to terms with the realization that I was part of his problem. Once I did that, I was able to remove the barrier between us, and I could see that he was listening. In his own way he had always been listening. There are no words to express my gratitude to you for what you have done for me.

One more thing I must tell you. It wasn't just a coincidence that we sat in those two seats, next to each other. You see, I had been praying for a miracle to come into my life. You, Jim, were my miracle and I thank you with all of my heart."

I expressed my appreciation for her comments and we spoke for several more minutes before saying goodbye.

After hanging up the phone, I stood by the window and listened to the sounds of the craftsman's tools as he worked in the house, and I began to compare the significance of the tools to the significance of life. Without the tools and the skills, the craftsman can't create the beauty he envisions in his mind. Without the understanding or the enlightenment, we can't create the beauty we seek in our lives.

When Michael told me that I had volunteered to help others reach enlightenment, this is what he had meant. I had volunteered to be the craftsman. Michael and Alea had been my teachers. They helped me shape and prepare the tools I use in the workshops and seminars to open hearts and touch souls.

The letters and e-mails I receive after doing a workshop are the direct result of the tools in the craftsman hands. One letter in particular that I received, stood out in my mind

"When I came to your workshop I did not know what I was in for. I thought my life was just fine. What I discovered was nothing short of a miracle. I am so grateful for all you did for me in helping me let go of some past issues. I don't know how you discovered what you have, but I think the whole world needs to know about it and I'm going to do my part in telling everyone I know."

How I discovered what I have, is a miracle itself. The gratitude I feel for two spiritual beings who stepped into my life and changed it, is so overwhelming at times my heart feels as if it is going to burst.

My own self-discovery continues, however, through the experiences I encounter every day. I held a three-day workshop right after Bella had been attacked by the doe. The emotion of that experience brought a clarity of heart and mind that I hadn't felt before, and it seemed to heighten my commitment to those who sat in the audience, and the mood of the workshop was felt with a deeper intensity.

As I began sorting my mail I recognized some of the names on the return address stickers from that workshop, and I picked up an envelope.

I took the letter out of its envelope, unfolded it and began to read.

"Your workshop has changed my life forever! I am unable to fully express the impact it had on me. I was in a state of sadness, anger, denial, depression, and didn't know which way to turn. Not any more, thanks to you, I let it all go."

I laid the letter on the desk, feeling good about what I had read, and opened the next letter.

"Thank you for your tremendous workshop. It was awesome. You have taken some ancient abstract philosophies and translated them into very practical, doable processes that everyone can master. I now find myself experiencing the magic of life flowing through me on multiple levels. I always think of the letting go process when times get tough. It always works! It's timed released enlightenment!"

I liked the phrase, timed released enlightenment. It was perfect.

Alea and Michael, I hope you can see the miracle of what you have done, and thank you for letting me be a part of it.

I was just opening the third letter when the phone rang again. This time it was Joanna.

"I'm coming home tomorrow. I'll be on the 1:00 pm flight. Will you be there to meet me?" Her voice sounded tired and strained.

"Are you alright?" I asked, controlling my own emotions. "Did your Mother pass away, then?"

"No, not yet. I don't know what is keeping her alive, but I need to come home for a while, then I'll come back if she needs me." Joanna was clearly crying now and I felt so helpless. "My brother left today, but Mom's friend will stay with her until I come back, so I'll see you tomorrow, ok?"

"I'll be there," I promised. We said our goodbye's and I hung up the phone. The mood in the office had changed and I sorted out and arranged everything into categories. I did what was absolutely necessary, then locked the office and walked toward the front of the house. I had forgotten to tell Joanna that the house was close to being finished. I'll tell her tomorrow.

As I rounded the corner Bella came running up to me. It was as if she sensed my need for company. We walked back to the trailer together and I fixed us lunch. I told her that Joanna was coming home tomorrow and she seemed content with the news.

The boys were clearly thrilled when I told them that their mother would be here when they got home from school the next day. We celebrated with my famous spaghetti dinner, which they had been served several times during the past three weeks. Even Walker liked it, and I could tell the extent of their excitement when they cheerfully went about their assigned responsibilities.

Walker suggested we all go to bed early so the time would pass faster.

By 10:00 pm, the laundry was all done and the trailer looked fit for Joanna's return. The boys were in bed while I sat in front of the TV trying to get sleepy.

My eyes were focused on the screen while my mind was focused on a disease that had taken the lives of my father and mother, my brother, my sister, Joanna's step-father, and now will be the cause of her mother's death. Cancer slowly stripped them all of life as they filled their lungs with the smoke of cigarettes. Ironically, as I sat there thinking, a commercial began its campaign.

A man was standing in the middle of the screen. *"I represent the major tobacco companies,"* he said. *"It has come to our attention, through years of clinical research, that cigarette smoking causes cancer, heart disease, and countless other health problems. For this reason, until we can develop a cigarette that isn't harmful to your health, we are going to recall all cigarettes that are currently on the store shelves."*

I couldn't believe what I was hearing. For a minute I thought I had fallen asleep and was dreaming. They are really going to do something about this? The TV screen faded to black and all was silent for a second. Then the man reappeared. As a smile spread across his face, he said, **"APRIL FOOLS."**

I sat there, stunned, allowing what I had heard to sink in. An extraordinary message had just been sent over the cable lines and through the satellite dishes, into millions of homes. How many, I wonder, actually felt the impact of the message as I had?

As I analyzed the words of the commercial I recognized its similarity, in part, to another commercial where Firestone announced a recall of over a million tires because of faulty treads. These tires were considered dangerous and had been blamed for hundreds of accidents, some with fatalities. It had been mandatory that Firestone recall those tires.

How many more millions of fatalities caused by cigarettes will have to occur before they will recall the cigarette? I had recently read somewhere that of the more than five-billion people alive today on earth, over one-billion would die from smoking. That's a billion people in the next sixty years or so! More people die from smoking each year than the combined deaths of all the wars in history. That is a shocking revelation.

I realize we each have to take the responsibility of our own actions but when something in a product is known to be so devastatingly harmful to the body, and yet the product is still offered to the public, the responsibility then must be shared. Tires are recalled, medication is recalled, cars are recalled, food is recalled, all because of something within their structure that is dangerous to the well-being of the people using them. When will they recall cigarettes? I wonder how many young people will be sucked into the use of this hideous drug because of the lack of education from parents about its deadly effects?

I suddenly felt the need sleep and turned off the TV. I closed my eyes and allowed myself to let go of the pain and sadness I felt for Joanna and her mom and I drifted into a quiet sleep.

Morning came with the regular routine the boys and I had set up, but this morning there was a different script. Both shoes were under the same side of Walker's bed, everyone had a drawer full of clean clothes and there were smiles on four faces as I handed them their lunches. I think the smiles were representation of one single thought, *"Monday, Mom will make my lunch, I can live with this one more day."*

When I got home from driving them to school, there was a message on the answering machine. It was Joanna's brother, Patrick, telling me to call him as soon as possible. I quickly dialed his number. He answered after the first ring.

"I know Joanna's plane is in the air right now and there is no way I can get in touch with her to tell her that Mom died not long after her flight left the ground." He said calmly though his voice was horse from fatigue. "I called the airport, but it was too late. There was no reason to have her go back to the hospital anyway, there was nothing for her to do."

"Thank you for calling me," I said. "Are you ok?"

"I think so," he replied, then he hesitated before going on to explain, "Kathy, who is Mom's best friend told me that it was as if she was waiting for everyone to leave so she could go. Joanna gave Mom a kiss this morning, and told her that she was going to fly home for a few days. She left and Kathy sat with her for a little while longer then she had a quick errand to run. Thinking Mom would probably sleep until she got back, she gave her a kiss and said 'goodbye', meaning she was going to be gone for a little while. However, I think Mom thought she was saying, goodbye, it's ok for you to go, and she died before Kathy reached the parking lot."

He paused for a moment then went on, "I've been thinking, maybe she was just hanging on for us. Maybe we were keeping her here and it wasn't until she was alone that she felt that she could die."

"That's a possibility," I said, "I'm just relieved that it is over for her, and for you and Joanna. Is there anything I can do for you?"

"I don't think so. Just tell Joanna I will contact the mortuary and make arrangements for the cremation. Joanna and I will go back out later and we'll take care of the ashes then. I'll give you a call when everything is done. Tell Joanna not to worry about anything. Right now she needs rest."

Joanna was the first passenger off the plane. I watched her as she walked toward me. She looked beautiful but exhausted. Her face was pale in spite of her makeup. Patrick had been right when he said she needed rest. As soon as a path was clear and I could get to her I held her in my arms, wanting so badly to take away some of the sadness she felt. I knew, however, that I would only add to it.

"I can hardly wait to see the boys," she said as I released her. "I have missed all of you so much."

"I think we've missed you more," I said, taking her travel bag from off her shoulder.

Once her luggage was stored in the trunk and we were on our way home she turned to me and said, "Tell me what you need to tell me."

I was amazed she could read me so well. I reached over and took her hand. "Your mother died this morning after your flight left Florida."

She laid her head back against the headrest and closed her eyes. Still clinging tightly to my hand, she said, "I wonder if she was staying alive just for me." Her eyes began to water with tears. "Do you think that's possible? Can a person will themselves to live even though they want to die, because of the love they feel for the person with them?"

"I think it is very possible." I answered.

"Maybe I should have come home a week ago for her sake."

"You don't know that for sure, Joanna. Maybe she wanted this past week with you."

"Do you know what makes me feel so bad?" she said as she wiped her eyes and stared out the side window. "She never talked about herself or her life all the time I sat with her. I wanted to hear about her childhood. I wanted her to tell me her deepest feelings. I wanted to hear her talk of things that made her happy and sad. I wanted to know her better before I lost her. I wanted more memories to hold onto. But she didn't talk, she didn't tell me what I longed to know.

I showed her the picture of the oak tree yesterday, and explained that is where we'll meet when I need to talk to her. She smiled at me, Jim, and promised she would be there whenever I needed her. For now, I will hold onto that."

"I had a dream one night, a few years ago," I said, recalling the memory. "In the dream I saw my father and mother. They were standing by me and I could feel my mother's hand in mine, and the warmth of my father's touch on my shoulder. They were smiling at me, and I felt they wanted me to know that they were together and were happy beyond anything I could comprehend. At the time I just thought of it as a dream but now I know different. She will be there, Joanna, I promise you."

Joanna's eyes closed then, her face was pale with fatigue and I thought she might sleep. A few minutes later, however, she sat up and stared out the windshield and words began pouring out once more.

"Kathy stayed right by Mom's side, with me. She talked of their friendship and how much she loved Mom. Did you know, Jim, that my mother influenced many lives because she was such a giving person?"

"I wouldn't be surprised, your mother had the gift of friendship," I answered.

She smiled at me, then continued, "Kathy would mention a name and tell me how Mom touched their life. Then she would mention another name and explain how Mom had made a difference in that person's life. It was incredible. I wonder if my mother knew of the good she had done just by being who she was?"

Then she was quiet again and I could tell she was struggling with something deep inside. Finally, the question worked its way to the surface. "I wonder," she sighed, "have I made a difference in someone's life? If I have, would I know?"

"In the past few weeks, I have learned a lot of things which I'll tell you all about later," I smiled. "But perhaps the most important thing I have learned is that your influence is the foundation of our home. You touch not only the lives of your sons but also the lives of other mothers as they watch you with your sons. You are an example they wish to emulate."

"And how do you know that?"

"Because I have listened and that is what I hear. People watch you, Joanna, and they see what a loving mother you are. They see your kindness and they are recipients of your generosity. If you need an answer to that question, I have it. The answer is, yes you have made a difference, not only in our lives but in the lives of many around you."

One example of her generosity came immediately to my mind. When we first moved to Grass Valley a few years ago, a woman had lost her husband and two children when a propane tank exploded in the trailer they were living in. One daughter had survived but was badly burned.

Joanna took it upon herself to organize a fund raising campaign to raise money to help this woman, whom she barely knew. She organized a local fair. She placed donation cans in stores all over the county with pictures of the family, asking everyone to help. Because of her deep sense of compassion for this woman and her family, she raised thousands of dollars to help pay medical and living expenses.

I reminded her of this example, then said, "That is one of the many reasons I love you so much."

She smiled at me, "Thank you for loving me so much."

It wasn't until I parked the car in the temporary driveway, that I realized I had failed to tell Joanna about the house.

"Oh, and I forgot to mention that the house is almost finished." I said as I helped her out of the car.

She looked in the direction of the house, blinked then looked again. "Oh Jim," she whispered as she grabbed my hand and walked me toward the house, "It's beautiful!"

Bella saw us coming and her greeting was a loud continuous bark. She showered Joanna with sprays of dust as she planted her paws on her pants, then down she went leaving two paw prints, and took her place as guide, and led us into the house.

Joanna went from room to room, touching the painted walls, checking the tile and taking in the view from each window. Her fatigue had been replaced with a childlike excitement. It was simply fun to watch.

"Here," she said, walking to the window in Weston's room, "is where we will plant the daffodils. When I think of daffodils I think of Weston, that's what I want to plant them beneath his window.

I smiled at Joanna as she talked about the daffodils. Weston had been three at the time and we were living in Sedona, Arizona. I remember it was February because some of the flowers were just starting to bloom.

I was in my office in the back of the house and working on a project for a company. I was supposed to be writing some brochures for them but nothing was flowing. I had been working for four hours and I had a deadline to meet.

The door was closed and Weston had been told that when the door was closed it means Dad is busy and if you have to come in then do it quietly.

A three-year old remembers instructions until something more important takes their place and he threw open the door, knocking it against the wall. He came running in and jumped up in front of my desk, his eyes big as saucers and he said. "Dad, come quick, come quick."

I looked at him in alarm. "What is it?" I asked.

"Ya gotta come quick, ya gotta come right now."

Again I said, "What's the matter?" I was sure something serious had happened.

He looked at me almost annoyed that I was taking so long to understand the importance of his message. "Ya gotta come now, Dad. Ya gotta see this."

I looked at my child in front of me and I saw the excitement in his eyes. I knew I had a deadline but I also have a deadline on Weston's childhood. I could take a few minutes for him.

He wrapped his little hand around my fingers and enthusiastically lead me down the hallway, down the front steps, down the driveway and down the street. I asked him, "Where are we going?"

All he would say is, "Come on Dad, you gotta see this."

There was a sidewalk that went to the back part of the property and on both sides there were flowers planted and he pulled me up to the sidewalk and stopped. He pointed down at the daffodils and said, "Look, Dad, the daffodils are blooming!"

We looked at the daffodils lined along the walk then he knelt down and motioned me to do the same. "Look inside the flower," he whispered with excitement. "What is it?"

"I don't know," was all I could reply. Looking at a daffodil with a three year old is a little bit different than just looking at one by yourself. I had never really looked at the part he was asking me about. Only a small child could take time to really look at and into a flower. Adults seem to be much too busy. But that day I spent ten minutes, not only looking at and into daffodils but also talking about daffodils. We looked at some that weren't open yet and he said, "When those open I'll come back and get you so you can see them too."

As I walked back to the house I shuttered slightly at the words I almost uttered, "Not right now, Weston, Dad's too busy. Maybe later."

Maybe Weston would have thought, "Well, my Dad's too busy, we'll look at daffodils later, or he might have walked away thinking, "My Dad's too busy and he's always too busy and the next time I see something pretty I'm not going to share it with him."

One thing I found out that day was that when you give your time to someone, you receive your time back with interest. When I sat down at my desk again, thoughts and ideas just started flooding through my mind and for the next thirty minutes I wrote and everything I put on paper worked.

I accepted a miracle and Weston was my messenger. He put me in a place of resourcefulness and love. That is where all answers are, where all things originate. In truth, I needed a break and he was the messenger of that truth.

"That is the perfect place to plant the daffodils," I said as I put my arms around Joanna and peered through the window.

It seems the world is full of miracles if we can just accept them as they happen. The miracle of life and of love together help to create a child. The miracle of sunshine and of rain help create a daffodil. The miracle of hope and of longing help create a path. The miracle of joy, and of sorrow, help create an understanding. The miracle of courage and faith help create the journey. We may choose to accept these things as miracles or we may not, it doesn't matter, they are here for us to use.

I, for one, believe in miracles. It was a miracle that introduced me to Michael and Alea. It was a miracle that introduced me to Joanna. I am surrounded by them every day as I comb a little boys hair, pack a lunch, or hug a tree. Each time I stand in front of an audience and watch the transformation in a person's life because of something they experienced that day, I witness a miracle.

I reached for Joanna's hand and smiled and together we started the walk back to the trailer. "Do you know what I think?" I asked her as we walked.

"I was wondering when you were going to share your thoughts," she laughed. I had missed her touch and the sound of her laughter. I added these to my list of miracles.

"I think your mother is happier today than she has been in years. I think she is where she wants to be. I think she loves you so much it was hard for her to leave you but grateful that you love her enough to let her go. I think death is part of the miracle of life."

"Thank you," Joanna said. Her face softened with relief as she put her arms around my waist and pulled me close to her. "I needed to hear that, I needed to know that coming home was the right thing to do."

I encircled her in my arms and I felt the tension leave her body as we looked into each other's eyes. A kiss seemed very appropriate here. I added it my list of miracles as I felt the warmth of her body and the tenderness of her kiss, which I always love.

When it was time to pick up the boys from school, Joanna insisted that she be the one to go. I didn't argue, my office really needed some attention, after being ignored for the most part for the past few weeks, and Joanna needed to be with her sons.

As I waved to Joanna and started toward the office, I noticed Bella had left the men on their own and found her favorite spot on my lounge chair to wait for her family to return. I gave her a pat and headed back to the work that waited on my desk. I decided to read one more letter before getting serious about the clutter on my desk. I picked one out of the stack, opened it and began to read.

"Your workshop has changed something within me. It's hard to explain, but I seem to be so much more in the moment and effective. The program was filled with revelations, discoveries and homecomings. The material was very useful and tremendous in its impact. I thought I would have to review it again, but I haven't, It has stuck with me. It continues to operate within me even weeks later."

Like the pedals as they entwine one with another and bring into existence an exquisite and breathtaking rose, miracles, in the form of discoveries and revelations entwine one with another to bring into existence an exquisite and breathtaking transformation.

Yet, with all the miracles in our lives, love is the master's key that brings it altogether and makes it work. This is my truth.

I sat in meditation and in the intimacy of the moment words began to place themselves in form within my mind. I picked up a pencil and began putting the words together on paper.

I had no time for stories, so much to do today,
My child sat with his toys, quietly at play.
He paused then, for a moment, picked up his ball and glove,
And softly asked the question, Daddy, what is love?

I knelt beside my little boy and put my arms around his waist.
I held him for a moment, not knowing what to say.
Then I looked at that little boy with his ball and glove,
I kissed him, and I said, "My child, you are love."

He put his face so close to mine, I could see deep in his eyes,
And there I saw a wisdom great, concealed in a child's disguise.
Then he put his little arms around my neck, still clutching that ball and glove,
He whispered reverently in my ear, "No my Daddy, you are love."

That day a knock came to my door, a stranger, tired, ragged and worn.
Stood on the step, his eyes were sad, he simply asked if he might get warm.
I welcomed him to sit and rest. He smiled at my child with his ball and his glove,
Then he said to me, "Sir, you are love."

WHAT I HAVE LEARNED FROM MY SIX SONS

I realized then, that he had given me more than I could give to him,
For he brought to me the gift of peace, this stranger, ragged, worn and thin.
And I reached out to the stranger, and my son held out his glove,
With humble heart, I said to him, "No, my friend, you are love

Now this day is ending and two loving arms embrace me.
My wife asks if she could share my thoughts, I kiss her tenderly.

This noble woman who shares with me, the owner of that ball and glove,
I answer in the words I've learned today, "My darling, you are love."

Then flows to my understanding, the strength and power from above
And from deep within my heart, I know that everyone is love.

I read the words I had written, one more time. It's the little things that make us happy, I decided. It's the little acts that change lives. A truly wealthy person needs very little to make him happy. Wealth does not come with a dollar sign. Wealth comes with love.

The excitement in Bella's bark told me her family was home once again. I folded the paper I had been writing on and placed it next to the picture of my four sons. Locked the door and made my way back down the path to the trailer.

Will was playing with Bella when I reached the trailer. "Grandma died today, Dad,"   he said softly, "but that is ok, because God will take care of her for us now, so we don't have to worry about her anymore." He looked up at me and smiled. "I think Grandpa is happier to see her come than we are sad to see her go."

"I think you are probably right," I smiled back at him.

Will, with his extraordinary ability to understand the spiritual element of life, could accept death without questioning the reason. Very few have this gift.

If daffodils are to be planted beneath Weston's window, I wonder where Joanna will find angel flowers to plant under Will's window or for that matter, cookie flowers to plant under Warren's window. I'm going to enjoy watching her ingenuity at work.

Warren seemed quiet throughout the evening and went to his room early. I think it was his way in dealing with his Grandmother's death. I felt a sense of compassion for him that compelled me to leave him alone. I didn't want to interfere with his ability to discover his own inner feelings. It was not for me to tell him what he should feel, only to respect that feeling.

Walker was curious about his Grandmother's death and asked his mother questions which she freely answered and he seemed content.

Weston took a rather mature approach. When I asked if he wanted to talk about it. He just said he was happy that his Grandmother didn't have to suffer anymore and that he loved her very much. I felt I didn't need to add to that.

For me, Joanna was home and that made everything right again.

The next morning brought with it the weekend, the sun, and the opportunity to sleep in which everyone took advantage of. Even the phone remained silent until 2:00 pm when Patrick called to tell us that everything had been taken care of. As he talked, he said something that really touched me.

"My mother lived sixty-one years," he explained, " and as Joanna I went through her home deciding what to do with her possessions, we found that everything that had value to us fit in one box. It's the memories that we treasure. It made me stop and think, if having possessions are the most important thing in life, then the whole meaning of life comes down to one box. The size of the box doesn't matter. What truly matters is that you lived and your life was a journey, and on that journey you made memories. On the journey you shared and experienced love, you developed relationships, you touched other's lives and allowed theirs to touch yours. It's about who you are and what you have done, not what you have acquired."

Patrick's words stayed with me. By observing the process of death he had figured out the pure essence of life in simple, yet profound words, and he was right.

I found Joanna sitting on my lounge chair so I slid her over and squeezed in beside her. "Do you know what I think?" I asked her.

"Do you know what I think?" she asked in return.

"What," I asked

"I think you and Will think alike."

I laughed, "No wonder I enjoy talking with him."

REFLECTIONS

Journal entry

A lot has happened in the Britt household these past few weeks. Where do I begin?

I honor a mother's world, for it is hallowed ground,
There her child is safe and warm.
Where fears are quieted with a simple hug.
Is it her touch that creates all beauty?

I am in awe of the understanding in my child's gaze.
Though inside his heart is breaking,
He knows the sorrows of others.
Is he wiser than me?

JIM BRITT

I recognize that miracles are the result of someone's prayer.
And life is not a just a coincidence, but an intelligence,
One life touching another.
How powerful is prayer?

I marvel at the ability of man to build a house.
With his tools, he carves and cuts, until, at last,
There stands a building of unique design.
Why am I not surprised?

I sense the truth of the tools in the craftsman's hand.
They bring to life the beauty of an open heart,
And timed released enlightenment.
Why am I so blessed?

I watched with sadness, as cancer stripped those I loved, of life.
How can a product so harmful to the body,
Have so much power over the mind?
When will they recall cigarettes?

I believe that death brings peace to those who suffer,
For death is one of the miracles of life.
And our circle is complete.
Why do we fear it so?

Though I will miss Joanna's mother I feel a sense of relief for her. I realize that I will always be grateful to her for her gift of friendship, a gift she graciously shared with me *by bringing her daughter into this world. We never know the value of such a gift until we are the recipient.*

I hear the voice of a three-year old calling, "Hurry Daddy, come quick."
And for the first time, I see a daffodil in bloom,
Because I took the time to kneel beside my child.
What if I had not listened?

I know it's the little things that make us happy,
It's the little acts that change our lives.
Wealth does not come with a dollar sign.
Why do we crave so much?

I've learned that what truly matters in life is that you have lived.
And that you made memories, and touched lives.
Life is about you, not what you have acquired.
Why can't we understand?

Thought for Today

The sadness is not to have died,
The sadness is not to have achieved
all that was within us to achieve.
While we lived

Chapter Nine

"Hey Dad," shouted a voice from far away, "come and see my room. I've got all my stuff out of the boxes. Boy, I forgot I had so much good stuff."

As I followed the sound of the voice, I found myself in Will's room where empty boxes had been stacked haphazardly in the doorway until, finally, they had no recourse but to spill into the hall, blocking the way for any further advancement. Once inside the room, however, I found almost perfect order, representative of a tidy eight-year old.

"Isn't it great!" he giggled as he carefully placed his scientific collection of rocks and fossils on a shelf. "My own room, and look how big it is. I could stay in here for days."

"It might take that long to find your way through the empty boxes stacked just outside your door," I laughed.

We were finally moving into our new house. I hadn't seen this much excitement since…well, I don't know if I have ever seen this much excitement. The house was ready to welcome us in, and every one of its inhabitants was emptying boxes by the ton, filling the empty spaces with things that mattered.

The storage company unloaded our furniture yesterday morning and since that time it had been non-stop excitement and work.

"Have you ever had so much fun?" Will asked as we inspected his room full of little boy things. Covering his bunk bed was a spread swirled with color and magical design. On the ceiling, hung the constellations, while the table held a lamp that, with the touch of the hand, produced the image of lightning. The dream catcher his Grandmother gave him just before she died, hung on his wall, just over his bed, and his keyboard set directly under it. I think I could stay in here for days, myself.

"You mean, have I ever had so much fun working?" I chuckled as I lowered my sore body into a chair in the corner of his room. I had to admit, however, I couldn't think of a time I had had so much fun working. Watching the walls come alive with pictures and the rooms warmed with furniture and plants had been fun. Sitting here in Will's room among the constellations and dream catchers, and surrounding myself with the colors and creations of his imagination really was, in the true sense of the word, fun! My greatest enjoyment, however, came from watching Joanna. She was like a whirlwind at play, and everything she added to the walls or the furniture brought brilliance into the room. I decided as I watched her magic, that it is, indeed, a mother's touch that creates all beauty.

As I sat, resting my sore muscles, I heard the phone ringing, then Joanna's voice. "It's for you, Jim. You can take it in the den, if you can find the phone." There was a slight pause, then she laughed, "On second thought, just come and use this one, it will save you a lot of time."

A few minutes later as I hung up, Joanna asked, "Are you going to be able to speak at the PTA Meeting next week?"

"You already knew they were going to ask me?"

"The PTA president talked to me yesterday," she replied as a smile crossed her face, "I told her it was you she would have to ask, although I knew you couldn't pass up an opportunity to speak unless you were already speaking somewhere else. So, are you speaking somewhere else or at the PTA Meeting?"

"It just so happens I am free next Thursday night or I was until I agreed to speak at a PTA Meeting. I do hope you plan to attend!"

"Wouldn't miss it."

The week progressed and our house began to take on the appearance of a real home. I began to feel the warmth and the love it now represented. The space seemed overwhelming at times after the confinement of the trailer, however, and I found myself missing the physical closeness we had shared for seven months. Here we would sometimes loose each other. Warren and Weston were happy to have the space and didn't seem to mind being lost in their own rooms.

Will and Walker aren't quite as eager to be so far away. A few days after showing me his room and telling me he could be happy just to be there for days, Will found me unpacking a box in my office. He sat on the floor next to me and said, "You know what, Dad? Sometimes I miss the trailer. We were closer together there. Sometimes, when I can't see you, I miss you and Mom, although I know you are here, you seem very far away."

"That's interesting, Will, I was just thinking the same thing." I said as I gave him a hug. "Sometimes, when I can't see you, I miss you too, even though I know you are just down the hall. The problem is that just down the hall is a lot further than it used to be."

Will smiled and secure in the knowledge that I felt as he felt, he was content. Bella's loud bark from the front of the house called to him, inviting him to come out and play, so with a quick 'high five', off he went in pursuit of the dog, and the outdoors.

My new office was big enough to hold everything I need and more. My large cluttered desk seems much smaller now. Perhaps, I thought, I should have two, one for the clutter and one for me.

As I emptied boxes and arranged furniture, my mind was free to work on the theme of the PTA assignment. By Tuesday, I was able to spend more time at my desk preparing, while Joanna took a much needed break. I watched as she walked down one of the many paths. She would take several steps and then turn and look at the house. A smile would appear on her face, then she would turn and walk again. Finally, she disappeared from my view, and I went back to the work in front of me.

In the next two hours things came together and I was beginning to feel confident with what I had prepared. I had just written down one final thought when the door opened and Joanna stood there, and though her face was serene, tears dotted her cheeks, unchecked.

"Come with me," she said softly as she held out her hand.

I could sense her emotion so, without questioning why, I rose from my chair, took her hand, and she led me outside. We walked in a reverent silence until we reached the old oak, then she stopped and motioned me to sit.

"She came," Joanna whispered as she knelt beside me. "She remembered and she came." Fresh tears glistened as they appeared in her eyes, and I reached over and gently wiped them away. I didn't speak. It wasn't my turn. I just listened as she told me of her mother's visit.

"I came to the oak tree not knowing what to expect," she began. "Wishing, hoping and wanting so much to feel her presence, but afraid I was asking too much, afraid I was expecting too much. I sat under the oak, closed my eyes, and in my heart, prayed she hadn't forgotten her promise, prayed she could fulfill her promise. I felt such a stillness around me, even the trees and the animals were quiet. The gentle music of the birds only added to the silence. Then, as if someone had placed a warm, healing blanket over me, peace entered my soul and she was there. I didn't even have to open my eyes to see her, I could see her in my heart.

She told me she knew of the sadness I felt because she had not spoken of her life before she died, then we talked of how she lived and how she died. We talked of the love we felt for each other and she asked me not to worry about her anymore. She is so happy, Jim. She is so happy. She told me that my step-dad wanted me to know of his love for me and he thinks we have wonderful children. Do you know that he already knows our children?"

Joanna, overcome with emotion, was quiet then, and she seemed to absorb herself in her own thoughts and in the miracle of what she had received. It was so quiet I could almost hear the silence of her thoughts and I let myself become the receptacle for her feelings.

As if she had suddenly remembered that I was there, she began to talk again. "My mother asked that we might do one thing for her, something she can no longer do herself. She asked that we protect our sons from the evils of smoking. She asked that we make sure they never put a cigarette to their lips. Her desire now is to save her grandchildren from the devastation smoking brings into a person's life. If what she has been through because she smoked will guard her grandchildren from even being tempted, then her death will have purpose."

Joanna moved closer to me and leaned her head on my shoulder. "I don't know if I will ever get to visit her again under the oak tree, but it's ok," she continued. "I know she is happy and that she loves me, and you, and our children so much that she would willingly go through it all again if it would shield us from the pain of the cancer she suffered because she smoked."

She raised her head and her eyes met mine, and, for the first time in weeks her eyes were clear and peaceful. Sadness had clouded them as she watched her mother die, and even the excitement of moving into her new home could not take the sadness from them. But, now, the strain had been lifted from her heart, her face, and her eyes. She looked as if she had experienced a transformation and maybe she had.

Now I know why I hadn't shared my experiences at the ball field and under the oak tree with Joanna before, I needed to wait until she could share hers with me. Now was the time. As she listened, she reached out, took my hand and enfold it safely in her own, and as I spoke, the feeling of love was so emotional I could hardly breathe. Once again there were no words eloquent enough or colors brilliant enough to define its beauty or intention.

We just sat under the tree, then, and I held Joanna in my arms and we were quiet. We didn't have to talk. There weren't any words to express how we felt. We were happy to live in the moment where nothing but love was present.

Tuesday afternoon, I watched as Joanna took Warren by the hand and led him to the oak tree. As they returned an hour later, Warren's arm was around his mother's shoulder and they were smiling. After the dinner dishes were cleared from the table, Joanna motioned to Weston and I watched once again as mother and son made their way to the oak. Wednesday afternoon, she took Will and Walker. With each one she talked about her visit with their grandmother, and of their grandmother's wish for them.

After the boys were in bed, Joanna and I sat on the patio just outside our bedroom and talked.

"They all loved her very much," she said, "and I believe each one of them felt their grandmother's love as we talked of her wish for them. It was a wonderful experience. Warren and Weston, of course, were the most affected by what I said to them and they each promised never to smoke. For Will and Walker, an explanation was almost unnecessary. They accepted the miracle of her visit as if it were a natural event. Will said he wished he could have been with me so he could tell his grandmother how much he missed her, and Walker asked if she knew we had moved into our new house." Joanna turned her face to me then, her forehead wrinkled into a playful frown. "They were both a little disturbed, however, that I should think they would even want to smoke an old dirty cigarette."

The moon was beginning to show itself and as we sat there breathing in the warmth of the night air, the stars slowly made their appearance.

"See my four stars," Joanna laughed. "They are right where I left them. I'm so glad I didn't lose them in the move."

Thursday evening came, and I was hoping I had everything I needed as we entered the room where the PTA Meeting was being held. It was almost full to capacity. The PTA President met us at the door and introduced herself to me. Joanna, of course, already knew her. She led us to our seats on a small portable stage and explained to me the order of the program.

"As you are the only speaker, you can take whatever time you need. These people have come to listen to you," She said as she handed me a program, "and I know they won't be disappointed. Thank you so much for coming, you don't know what this means to us." She smiled then, and turned to start the meeting.

After the official business was concluded and with my introduction I took my place in front of the microphone and found myself face to face with parents who wanted to make school a positive experience for their children, parents who cared about education and wanted the best for their children, parents who simply wanted to understand their children and needed support in learning the process. I decided after my talk I would open the floor to questions and answers. That way we could all learn from each other.

"First I want to tell you that I have come here to learn just as you have," I said as I viewed the audience, "only I get a lot more time to express my opinion. That may be a plus or a minus depending on how this school grades."

The audience laughed and I relaxed a little as I continued, "I remember the agonies of the first grade, where we were teased or made fun of in the midst of our innocence. We have all struggled in one way or the other to hide something about ourselves. I was taller than the rest of the class and I felt different, separate and alone. I was the only kid in the first grade with red hair and quickly was given the nickname, 'Red', which I detested. At the time I thought I was the only kid who felt that way, yet, how many of you have a story like mine?" Almost every hand in the audience went up as heads nodded. "It's not a conspiracy of some kind. We just all go through it in one way or another. It's simply a transition, an inevitable, sometimes painful passage from just knowing ourselves, to knowing the world around us. The real tragedy is that many of us never talk about our feelings, so we are never told that our 'red hair' is beautiful or that we don't need to hide or feel bad about ourselves no matter what anyone says at recess, therefore, we conclude that in order to live in the world, we must hide ourselves. Nothing could be further from the truth. To hide from truth, to believe even for a brief moment that we are not enough, is to hide from the love, joy and happiness we were meant to experience in life."

I asked the audience to help me make a list of the traits of small children. After a brief silence, someone said. "Innocent." I turned to the portable chalkboard and, with the chalk, wrote the word, *innocent*.

Another voice from the audience responded, "I think children are naturally happy and loving."

"Very good," I said as I wrote the two words on the board.

"Curious and spontaneous and perhaps a little fearless," a gentleman on the second row remarked.

I added these words to the list, and the list grew with other words like, playful, mischievous, exciting and beautiful. After reading over the list one more time, I looked at the audience and said, "We have to take note here. Shouldn't we be learning from our youngsters?" There was silence for a second as the audience was grasping my meaning, then heads began to nod in agreement.

"At some point in our lives," I continued, "we make a decision to become something less than who we are. We take on an identity, a role, and begin to cover up who we really are with who we 'think' we are. Then, after some time, we forget who we really are and begin to identify with, and think that who we think we are, is really who we are."

A hand went up and a voice asked, "Would you mind repeating that again for those of us who couldn't keep up the first time around?"

The audience chuckled and I repeated the phrase again.

"Got it this time, thanks, and I do believe you are right," responded the woman who had raised her hand.

The audience seemed to agree, and I continued, "To take it another step, we don't even like our new identity, but we have begun to forget our real self. We don't want others to know who we've become, so we take on even another identity, 'who we want others to think we are.' We gloss over with frills and glitter, who we are and who we think we are and who we've become and what we have. A sub-personality is then born, one that judges ourselves for not being enough, for not having enough.

Our whole life is then spent trying to reclaim our original identity - our true self, where love and happiness exist."

My eyes glanced over the audience as I finished this sentence and I saw an array of expressions. Some faces showed deep thought while others showed recognition and awakening. There were smiles and nods and a few frowns.

"My hope is that we can rediscover these wonderful traits in ourselves that we see in our children. Once we have made this rediscovery we can let go of what we think we are and become once again the person we are, letting ourselves become better parents. We then, in turn, complete the cycle by teaching our children, and allowing them to be who they really are."

I spoke for several more minutes about parenting and then opened the floor for questions.

Several hands went up immediately. A young man, I would guess, about thirty-five years old responded as I pointed to him.

"I believe we all know that we need to take a different approach to parenting today than our parents did twenty-five to thirty years ago," he responded, then asked, "Where do we begin?"

"It all begins with leadership. A parent is a leader," I explained. "Leadership is having the courage to be first. Courage, meaning 'strength of heart'. The first step is knowing that if we are going to raise healthy, productive children, we need to do something differently. Courage is sort of a threshold. You see a house on fire and a child trapped inside. There is a choice. You can choose to enter the burning house or not. Do we speak our truth...or not? Do we stand before ourselves without illusion...or not? Do we do what's best for our children...or not?

There is another kind of courage. After running into the burning house to save the child, the courageous person is puzzled to be considered brave. They often say, 'I had no choice, I had to run into the burning building to save the life of the child.' Is it not as important, then, to take on the leadership role and to have the courage to take action to make a difference in how our children are raised. Is there a choice when it comes to saving the life of a child who is trapped in a circumstance beyond their control.

Despite the consequences and the criticism of the modern day philosophy, true leadership and true courage are honoring what you know to be true, from the deepest core of your being. At this level, there is more than just a summoning of willpower, but rather a following of true knowledge.

But, if we are to teach our children the correct principles, we first must understand and have the courage to live by those same principles. That is where we as parent-leaders must begin.

Some may think your choice is illogical and, in that case, it may require a bit more courage to stand firm for what you know to be true. You may even be condemned as selfish for seeking the truth. Einstein once said that the enlightened individual will experience great irritation from the mediocre minds. Real leadership is having the courage to stick to your values and rise above the opinions of others.

Having answered the question to the best of my ability, I asked if there were any more questions. The audience was ready. Once again I had to choose from several hands.

"What is the most important element when it comes to disciplining a child?"

"Patience, patience and more patience," I answered to the chuckling audience. "It's the antidote to anger, which is based in fear. Fear wants us to act too soon, but patience, as difficult as it is sometimes, helps us to outlast our preconceptions. Given enough time, most of our problems and conflicts cease to be problems and conflicts because waiting will allow us to see ourselves in them, as part of them. When using anger or force with the child, what the parent is really doing, unknowingly, is turning his back on the child, and on the real issue.

There is a natural law that never fails, one that always works the same way every time it is in use. It is called the law of 'cause and effect'. Let's say, for example, that a parent is filled with anger. What will happen is their children will appear to them to be more hostile and misbehaving, which creates more anger on the part of the parent and more misbehaving on the part of the child...the law of cause and effect. When the parent makes the choice to move toward love by letting go of their anger and applying the antidote, patience, instead of choosing the temporary pleasure from being 'right', only then can the conflict in the relationship be healed.

No matter how you slice it, anger is an act of violence. A little anger is a little violence. A lot of anger is a lot of violence. And no matter how you perceive it, violence is abuse. And abuse should never be used to discipline a child, or to resolve any problem for that matter. Violence is never the answer, whether dealing with a child, your spouse, or a conflict between two countries.

Patience will reveal the truth and the truth is that it takes two to have conflict. In essence, when we are angry with another, we are angry with ourselves. No one can 'make' you angry. It's up to you, and only you can determine how you react or respond. When we distrust another, we distrust ourselves. When we hurt another, we hurt ourselves. When we abuse another verbally, we abuse ourselves. So when we feel angry, hurt or betrayed by our child, as difficult as it is, just wait and more often than not, you'll see the beauty in things as they are. Only then can you know exactly the appropriate, loving, action to take for the good of all.

A problem or conflict can be resolved much faster by using the power of love rather than the power of the ego. Our children are the messengers of love, and it's our job as parents and adults to help them carry that message through to the next generation.

A child's mission, when he or she is born, is to be completely and openly who they are. As parents, our job, as I see it, is not to discipline and to correct as many parents believe, but rather to love and guide our children, keeping the channel of love open in them, and between us, allowing them to unfold naturally into who they were meant to be."

Our children are not our children. They are God's children. We are simply their caretakers, their guides. Our job as parents is to help them to remain the joyful beings they are when they arrive here on this planet until they become young adults.

Think, for a moment, how you were raised. Did discipline in the form of anger or abuse ever get in the way of love or even get misinterpreted as love? Our parents did the very best they could, with the knowledge and experiences they gained from their own upbringing. It didn't mean that there wasn't a better way. It simply meant they didn't know a better way. Love is the way. It's time for us to break the chain of pain and create a new generation of World leaders.

Just as a river is shaped by the water that moves through it, children are continually shaped by the love, the feelings and experiences that move through them. If there is no water moving through the river it will eventually dry up and harden. On the other hand, the miracle of love is that it fills whatever it touches causing it to grow while leaving traces of its touch. As parents we leave traces of our influence, what flows from us, upon our children as they grow.

A child is simply a reflection of his or her parents. If a child is troubled in some way, the first place we should look is within ourselves.

A hand from the back of the room went up immediately and the question was asked, "Don't you think we confuse our children when we begin to compare them to their siblings, diminishing their own character?"

"Thank you for that question," I responded, and asked in return, "How many of you have been compared to a younger or older sibling at some point in your life?"

More hands than I had anticipated went up.

"I won't ask how many of you have compared your own children, but think how it made you feel when it happened to you. In a way, comparing a child to their older or younger siblings is another form of abuse. Doing so belittles the child, destroys their self-esteem and self-wroth as well as creates conflict between the siblings. The child looks to their parent, who they love and trust, for guidance. When the parent compares one child to another, the parent is, in essence, telling the child they are less of a person than the other in some way. Instead of comparing we should celebrate the differences in our children and nurture those individual qualities they possess.

"How do you keep the connection with your child as they grow older?" asked a woman from somewhere in the middle of the rows of chairs.

"Touch. Simply by touching," I said. "There are many reasons we need to be touched. The most profound is that we want to be emotionally healed. We all crave that comforting touch when the pain and confusion of living becomes too great to bear alone. A loving touch can relieve a heavy burden.

When a child feels alone and doesn't know where to turn for the answers, they crave the touch, the hug from a loving parent to make things good again. Touch transcends all languages. It is an energy that connects all that lives inside our hearts.

We can disagree about many things. You could be Christian or Hindu, man or woman, live in a city or rural area, but all the walls between us will crumble by the touch of a compassionate, gentle hand. Even as adults we all crave touch.

The need for a parent to touch or hug their child should never be in question or never be withheld any more than we question or withhold our need to breathe. Touch has a healing language of comfort that is universally understood. Hug your children often. Hug each other often."

There was time for one more question and without raising his hand, a gentleman on the front row said, "It seems that since they have taken prayer out of the schools, respect and discipline followed through the same door. I'd like to ask two questions. First, are you a Christian and second, do you think religion has a place in the school?"

I hesitated for a brief moment to gather my thoughts before answering. I always felt when asked if I was a Christian, I was about to be judged as being good or bad, right or wrong. I decided all I could do was speak from my heart.

"Before I answer that question," I responded, "let me ask how many of you are Christians?"

Though the audience looked a little surprised, almost half of them raised their hands.

"How many of you are Jewish?"

Twelve hands went up.

"How many Buddhist?"

Eighteen hands were raised."

With every person who raised their hand came the affirmation of their religious belief.

"Though you may be called Jewish, Christian, Buddhist or Hindu, when we get to the core we are all the same. Our beliefs may vary to a certain degree but one thing we all believe in is a Supreme Being who guides and influences our lives. We are each like a spoke in a huge wheel, all coming together in a common place and discussing ways to enhance the good of all. In the deepest core of our being, no matter what our religion, we care for all souls, don't we?

In a way, I consider myself all of these religions. I meditate, therefore, I am Buddhist. The Jewish celebrate 'Tashleek,' which means to release all your worries of the past year, a letting go, therefore, I am Jewish. I don't drink coffee, that makes me a Mormon." I smiled at my one Mormon friend in the audience and winked. She rolled her eyes and smiled back. "I believe in living in the present moment, therefore, I am a Buddhist. I pray, therefore, I am Christian. To judge another for not believing what I do would be to judge myself for not being open to seeing the truth. The truth is that there is value in all religions.

To answer your question, yes, I believe religion has a place in the schools. I believe respect for every religion should be taught as well as respect for every culture. It is how our children learn tolerance and acceptance.

We are like a huge grove of aspen trees growing beside the river. Each tree appears to be growing independently, but beneath the surface, there lies a massive root structure in which they are all intertwined and intimately connected to the well-being of each other. Once we realize this, we have no choice but to embrace the well-being of our neighbors as part of our own well-being. When we judge even a stranger for what they believe or don't believe, we are cutting ourselves off from the very core of existence. When we don't embrace others, we stifle our own growth. When we love all life, we love ourselves in return.

In a very deep sense, when we heal ourselves, we heal the world in which we live. Live on purpose, take responsibility for your part. Care for your own life as if it were the whole world. That is my religion in a nutshell. So I say that we should take a risk and openly give thanks for all people, personalities, and all religions. We should allow ourselves to feel and let all that is living touch our hearts. Do not hide who you are and guard yourself against pain, but rather be who you are and remain open to all that can heal you.

It takes courage, as I mentioned at the beginning, a 'strength of heart', to do this, but in order to raise our children in this modern world, that is what it will take. We must become leaders and live as the example so that our children can know the way.

Mother Teresa put it very simply when she said; "*If you find serenity and happiness, others may be jealous, be happy anyway. The good you do today, people will often forget tomorrow, do good anyway. Give the world the best you have, and it may never be enough, give the world the best you have anyway. You see, in the final analysis, it is between you and God, it was never between you and them anyway.*"

As I conclude my talk I just want to remind you that Einstein was four years old before he could speak and seven before he could read. Isaac Newton did poorly in grade school. A newspaper editor fired Walt Disney because he had 'no good ideas'. Beethoven's music teacher once said, 'As a composer, he is hopeless'. Henry Ford quite school at the age of sixteen, and Winston Churchill failed the 6th grade. Never, never give up on your child. Great things can happen to them if they don't give up. More importantly, great things can happen to your children if you don't give up on them."

As I sat down, the audience rewarded me with a sounding round of applause for which I was grateful. Having the courage to speak from the heart sometimes takes a lot of energy.

"You were very impressive," Joanna said, as we got into the car for the ride home. "The people really liked what they heard tonight. I watched their faces as you spoke, and saw their expressions of appreciation as well as that look of awakening to the ideas you presented to them. Then, of course, I was busy accepting accolades in your behalf while you were talking to the PTA Board after." She laughed, then reached over and brushed a kiss across my cheek. "That's for taking the time to speak to people who want nothing more than to be successful in their responsibility as parents. In fact, many of them took notes but asked if they could have a copy of your talk. I recorded it and I said you would be more than happy to give them a copy. I made a list of the names, and I'll make sure the copies get to them for you."

I reached my arm around her and brought her close to me. She was my life, my most valiant ally, and I would be empty without her. "Would you make sure the PTA President gets a copy also, she asked if I would speak at their State PTA Board Meeting in September. I think I received an 'A-' for my presentation."

"An A+ is more like it," Joanna looked at me in surprise. "Why would you say an A-?"

"One man sitting in the middle of the fifth row, left hand side, slept almost all the way through the meeting," I laughed, "so in calculating, I didn't get one-hundred percent."

"Maybe he was visualizing,"

"Or, maybe he was sleeping."

"Maybe he was listening with his eyes closed."

"Or, maybe he was sleeping."

"Maybe, it didn't make any difference in your grade because you graduated with honors, tonight," she giggled.

As we turned onto our property we could see the house, lighted against the darkness of the sky. The moon was full and bounced a soft glow across the tops of the wooden beams that extended out beneath the flat roof.

"Oh Jim, our home is even more beautiful at night," Joanna sighed.

The lights were on inside, extending a warm, welcome feeling to us as we drove in the driveway. It was good to be home.

The next day brought the end to the boxes and the furniture was all in place, so we had time to spend outside. Joanna and I decided a family picnic at the river would be an appropriate celebration for the occasion, so as a family we packed the picnic basket full of whatever we wanted and after stopping for a blanket, we were off to the river.

Bella was as happy as the rest of us to see an end to boxes and showed her approval by jumping and barking as we stepped off the porch, demanding attention. Will and Walker were her main targets, they quickly got the message and ran after her.

"Look," Warren said, pointing to the right, just beyond the house, "five little fawns just beyond the fence, can you see them?"

Just as we turned our gaze toward the fence, one little fawn jumped over and into the yard. As she landed, Bella came around the opposite side of the house chasing after Will, Walker not far behind. As soon as she spotted the fawn, she straightened her course and came directly toward the fawn, barking excitingly. The frightened fawn made a sharp turn and ran, with Bella at her heels. I shouted to Bella, trying to call her back, but she paid no attention to my command and continued in her chase.

Just as she got close to the fawn, a doe leaped the fence in defense. Bella let her attention turn from the fawn to the doe and I could see, in that split second she remembered the last time she met with a doe. She came to a screeching halt, made a one-hundred and eighty degree turn, and with a frightened look in her eyes, she ran in the opposite direction, the doe right behind her with a glare of determination that she was going to get this dog.

She chased Bella around the house before I could get in front of her and wave my arms to scare her off. Once I could get her attention, she veered to the left and bounded back over the fence and into the woods, keeping the fawns close to her.

Bella, with her tail between her legs and her head hanging, staggered onto the porch where she sought safety on my favorite lounge chair. Walker was beside her in an instance, scolding her for chasing the fawn, then hugging her because she was shaking. He was shaking almost as much. Will and Weston were by her side, showering her with sympathy and chastising her at the same time. Their faces were as pale as Walker's.

"I think," said Warren, "Bella may have learned her lesson."

"I hope so," I replied. Joanna walked over to Bella and patted her head. She looked up at her with big, sad eyes and whimpered what she considered to be an apology. She accepted it graciously and invited her to walk with us.

Her recovery was quick and before long she was running ahead of us then circling back behind. We were off to the short walk to the river. By the time we reached the river, Bella was searching for something smaller than a fawn to chase. As she was sniffing the ground, a squirrel crossed her path and she was off in pursuit. In a couple minutes, though, she lost interest in the squirrel because swimming in the river was her most favorite thing to do. She was first to dive in followed by Warren, Weston, Walker, and then Will about five minutes later. Will was always a bit more cautious when it came to jumping in the river.

We found the perfect spot between two pine trees and spread the blanket down, opened the basket and brought out the food.

"So what are we going to do with all our property, Dad?" asked Will in between bites of his peanut butter sandwich.

"First of all," I answered, "we don't want to disturb the pines and oaks but we do need to cut out all the scrubs. After that, we will level the area near the house to plant some ground cover. Then…,"

"When you say 'we', how many we's are we talking about?" Warren asked. "Are we talking 'we' as in you, me, Weston, Will and Walker, or are you talking 'we' in a general sense and someone else will be doing the big work?"

"A little of both, I suppose," I smiled. "You remember that green area near the front of the property?"

"Yes" Warren nodded. "The reason it stays so green is because there is a natural spring beneath it, so we will dig down and make a pond or, for your sake, Warren, we will have a digger come and dig the pond."

"Thanks Dad, I know my muscles will appreciate that."

"Cool," said Will, who was born to be wet. "That will give us three ponds. I like that idea."

"I thought you would," I smiled. "But mostly, we will leave the property in its natural state for which Bella will be truly grateful."

"What about the snakes?" asked Walker. "Will we build a fence for the snakes and let them be a part of the natural habitat?"

"We found a baby rattler near the pond on the back of the property, yesterday," Weston said. "We knew if it was there, the mother snake couldn't be too far behind. I vote we don't consider them part of the natural habitat."

Warren and Will cast their votes with Weston.

"We are still waiting for a reply to our letter we sent concerning the control of snakes," Joanna said, not wanting to vote against Walker's snakes but not wanting to content with them either, "so let's table that one until we have more information."

All were in agreement, the picnic basket was almost empty of food by now, and it seemed like a good time to just lay back on the blanket and relax and watch the boys and Bella swim. The plan was good but Bella's bark accompanied immediately with a shrill whine that grew louder as she made her way toward us, changed everything. Before we could even react, there she was, almost on top of us.

"Oh no," shouted Warren, sniffing the air, "she's been sprayed by a skunk, everybody run!"

The sickening odor of the skunk's perfume was suffocating even before Bella planted herself in the middle of the blanket, knocking over the picnic basket and spilling its contents all over her, the blanket and the ground.

We all just stood as far away as possible and watched while she kept pawing at her nose, desperate to remove the smell that clung to her.

"Who's in charge here?" asked Joanna, backing away a little further and holding a napkin tightly against her nose.

"Not me!" shouted Warren

"Not me either," shouted Weston.

Will and Walker were nowhere to be seen.

"Not me, either," I echoed.

"Reminds me of the story 'The Little Red Hen'," Joanna said, her voice choking with the fumes, "Ok, I'll be in charge."

"Let's pack up and head back home" ordered Joanna. Within two hours, the dog had been bathed in tomato juice, vinegar and soap, then sprayed with the hose. The blanket, the basket and anything that had touched Bella, had been buried. Everyone had showered and the clothes were in the washer that were redeemable.

Bella is now sitting in my favorite lounge chair, every once in while snorting the air. Walker is sitting beside her reading a story to make her feel better.

"I wish I could get that kind of attention when I do something wrong," laughed Warren. "Somehow it seems the punishment was handed out to the innocent in this case."

"Sometimes that happens," I replied, "when you have a dog who confuses a skunk for a squirrel.

As I watched Walker gently stroking Bella as he read to her, I began to wonder how many parents would hold their child that gently and read to them after he or she had done something wrong. Would there, instead be strong, painful, hurting words hurled or worse, the strike of a hand, for the stupidity of the act in the eyes of the parent. I could only conclude with this question. If a parent could treat their child with as much love and understanding when a mistake is made, as they treat their dog, what kind of children would they raise?

"I don't think," I said, nodding toward the touching scene in my lounge chair, "that you would be willing to get sprayed by a skunk just so Walker would stroke your hair and read to you."

"You have a point there," he laughed.

What I'm wondering is how to get the skunk scent out of my nostrils."

"Well," teased Warren, "you could follow Bella's example and try snorting,"

I wasn't really into snorting so I lit the citronella candle Joanna had set on the small table, then peeled and shared the orange she left beside the candle, with Warren. We both munched quietly on the orange slices and listened to Walker read the other version of "The Little Red Hen" to Bella. As his voice imitated the different animals, we relaxed and we felt better too.

"Not I," said the duck.

"Not I," said the pig.

"Not I," said the dog.

REFLECTIONS

Journal Entry

I've learned that a dog's nose sensors aren't refined enough to capture the scent of a skunk before the skunk can capture the dog with its scent.

I've learned that the story of "The Little Red Hen" can be revised in an instant.

I've learned that moving can be fun as soon as I began to view it through Will's eyes. He saw adventure, and adventure is what it should be. My muscles, however, failed to recognize the fun and continued to complain.

> *I walked into a house, it's walls were cold and bare.*
> *Every room was empty, I heard no voices there.*
> *The bare floors echoed and I felt the silence ring,*
> *I heard no warm, inviting sounds, little children bring.*
> *I wondered to myself, what makes a house a home?*

WHAT I HAVE LEARNED FROM MY SIX SONS

Then I watched as rooms began to fill with things that matter most.
I looked and saw the smiling face of a loving, gracious host.
I heard the children's laughter and the bark of a friendly dog
Each sending out the message of a happy monologue
Now I know what makes a house a home.

Near our home stands an old oak tree that has taken on the status of "the family tree." It's the tree I like to hug. It's the tree Walker sits under to study books about snakes. Weston and I discussed energy as we rested beneath its shade, and it was under that same oak tree that Joanna communicated with her mother shortly after her mother's death.

I believe a thin veil shields the Heavens from us.
yet, oft times love, in its divinity and grace,
Can allow us, even just for one brief moment
An opportunity to see beyond this time and space.

There to sit beside the one we've longed for,
The one who now resides beyond the veil
And listen to the words we've wept for
And, finally know that all is well,

Joanna's mother's wish that we teach her grandsons about the devastating dangers of smoking reiterated my discovery that our best teachers are our children themselves, if we will just listen.

Children are naturally innocent,
Mischievous and playful.
They are born loving,
Exciting and beautiful.

By nature, they are happy
Inquisitive and curious
And children are fearless
Joyful and spontaneous.
Shouldn't we listen to our children!

When innocence is exchanged
For identities not their own
And natural beauty is hidden
For fear of being alone.

When excitement is smothered
And curiosity spawns regret
Then fear replaces fearlessness,
As they reach for a cigarette
Shouldn't we have listened to our children!

Thought for today

All I may achieve in the eyes of men
Means nothing.
If I have achieved nothing
In the eyes of a child

Chapter Ten

Once again I am sitting here at my cluttered desk. It isn't any cleaner now than it was before I moved into my new office. I had told myself that once I was really permanent, I would have a clean desk because there would be a place for everything. Even in this spacious room, with a place for everything, my desk looks the same. I could blame it on the fact that I've been in Florida for the past week, but I doubt that would fly. The only acceptable conclusion I can come to is that I prefer a cluttered desk.

Just over six years ago, Joanna's stepfather, Johnny, who had been a fisherman by trade and a lover of the sea by preference, had requested that when he died, his ashes be spread near his favorite fishing hole off Conch Key, Florida. He had written down the exact coordinates for this event, and passed away shortly after. It had been an emotional experience as we followed the instructions etched on a piece of paper in his handwriting.

A week ago, six years later, to the exact date that we spread his ashes, Patrick and his Yolonda; Kathy and her husband, Ray, met Joanna and I in Conch Key, where we sailed out to the same spot, and in a reverent and private ceremony, silently spread the ashes of a wife, a mother and a friend whose life had touched so many and was now free to be with the husband who was waiting for her.

Roses were spread across the water in remembrance of the memories she left behind, then we quietly listening to the sound of the waves slapping the boat, as we watched the current carry the roses out of sight, allowing the silent tears to flow freely. We sat for twenty minutes not wanting to disturb the love that surrounded us. It was an extremely moving experience.

Then, as if by the wisp of the wind, the solemn mood was lifted and the breeze whispered, "Don't linger, get on with life."

The rest of the day we did just that. The boat was steered to Johnny's favorite fishing hole and we laughed and talked of things of the past and hopes for the future, and we fished.

I hadn't met Ray until the day before, and I wanted to get to know him better so while we sat, waiting for the fish to bite he told me his remarkable story.

"I had my own sevent- foot boat and I had money enough to do whatever I wanted to do," he began. "But in time it didn't seem like enough, so I began hanging out with what I considered to be the 'cool' guys. They drank so I drank, and, little by little, I began drinking more and more. They used cocaine so I began to use cocaine, and, little by little, I began to use the drug more and more, until I found myself just living for the next high.

It was all so subtle, going from one life to the other, happening just a little at a time, and I had not recognized the destruction until it was too late. My money was gone, I had to sell my boat to support my habit, and finally, I found myself homeless. I didn't know where to go, because I had nowhere to go.

One day, it was raining. I was shivering from the cold, and searching for a place of protection from the storm. In my search I found the Mangrove trees. It had become a home for the homeless like myself, an alcoholic and a druggy. It was a scary place to live. Everyone there needed the same thing I did and would steal or kill to get the money for their next fix.

Then, one day, just seven years ago, when I was sober enough to take a look at my life, I asked myself, 'what are you doing?' Then, I turned and walked away from it. I was able to clean myself up so I could look for a job. For some reason, I was blessed enough to meet your Mother-in-law, who sponsored me into AA, and several of the right kind of people who helped me. Soon, I was able, once again, to start my own business. Then I met Kathy, we got married five years ago, and look at my life now." We are both very happy.

"What an incredible story," I said, impressed by this man sitting beside me.

"I've read your book, 'Rings of Truth', and I am an example of what you teach." He smiled as he spoke. "I had to see myself as I really was, then I had to decide for myself what was really important and once I was able to open my mind and my heart, I became what you describe in your book as resourceful, and I conquered the beast. And, now you see the rest of the story, as Paul Harvey would say."

That was a week ago and, today I sit at my desk writing Ray's story just as he had told it to me while it was still fresh in my mind, so I could add it to my files.

It had been a remarkable week in Florida. The feelings we had experienced as we sat in the boat needed to be remembered, and the friendships we shared should not be forgotten.

I leaned my head against the back of my chair and thought of Joanna and what we have together. As my mind concentrated on her, my eyes drifted from my desk to the walls around me and I could see Joanna, or rather her influence, everywhere in the room. She had taken a picture of her and me on our first date and had it mounted and framed. It is now hanging on the wall. There is greenery and pottery on the shelves around the room and Southwestern art on the wall to my right. On the left, three large files fill the space. On top of the files, in chronological order, my journals are supported by two large bookends. A new family portrait watches over me from the wall just above the journals. Everything is very neat and orderly except my desk, which, I think, gives contrast to the room and makes it feel comfortable.

Feeling completely exonerated I turned on my computer in preparation for work. While I was waiting for it to warm up, Warren stepped inside the door.

"Got a minute, Dad?" he asked.

"At least that," I chuckled, "I'm warming up the computer. Come on in and have a seat. As you can see there is no room on the desk, but I do have a few nice, empty chairs."

He glanced at my desk as he slid a chair up next to it. "I've read that creative people prefer cluttered desks, maybe you fit into that category," he smiled as he gave me a wink, then he added, "It kind of gives contrast to the neat stuff Mom has done to the room though, don't you think?"

"I was just thinking that, myself, thank you."

Warren's eyes grew serious as he leaned back on his chair. "Remember when we talked about happiness and pleasure a couple of months ago, and you said that if I could make a difference in just one life, I will have made a difference in the world?"

I nodded. I had been looking forward to this conversation with great anticipation.

"Well, I made the decision in my mind to do what you suggested. At first I was concerned that the guys would try and get me to do the drugs and, in the beginning, a few of them offered, but when I refused, they didn't push the issue, and actually made sure no one else did. Two of them were kids I knew from little league. One of them, whose name is Anthony, had been an all-star two years in a row. He was a great baseball player, Dad, and he got kicked off the high school team this year for using drugs. He knew he shouldn't be doing that stuff and he knew the consequences, yet he let it suck him in."

WHAT I HAVE LEARNED FROM MY SIX SONS

Warren leaned forward on the chair and rested his elbows on the desk, "I remembered you telling us about the law of 'cause and effect,' that if there are certain things you don't want to happen, the best way to insure that they don't happen is to make sure the condition that would cause the event to take place doesn't happen. You explained that it is a natural law that never fails, and it works the same way every time it is applied."

"That's correct, go on."

"At first I didn't think much about it, but then I saw the law in action and I really wanted to help Anthony for some reason. I could see that he didn't really want to be part of the scene he continually allowed himself to be drawn into that led to the very thing he didn't want to do, but he didn't have the courage to step away from it, so I decided that I would test the law by using it to reverse the cycle.

I would give him choice to come with me and do something else instead of doing the drugs. At first, I wasn't very successful, but I continued to offer him a choice and, one day, he accepted the offer. We spent the afternoon playing catch. The next time we went to a movie and had burgers after. The third time, he asked me why I cared? I told him because I was his friend. From that point, it was as if a change had taken place inside of him and he was no longer afraid to say 'no' to the guys."

Warren paused and stood up, then he walked to the window and looked out toward the oaks and I could sense the emotion in his voice as he continued, "One day Anthony told me how he got started with the drugs and then he expressed his appreciation to me for what I had done for him. He even cried, Dad, so I cried with him. Then, do you know what we did? We hugged a tree! I explained to him the importance of tree hugging and we hugged a tree. It was like all of the stuff he had been carrying around for so long was lifted from him and he could laugh. He's going to play on the summer baseball league, then he hopes to try-out for the University team. I think he'll make it because now he is willing to do what it takes to make it.

You were right. Because I cared I made a difference. Now Anthony wants to do the same for someone else, so we are going to start working on Smitty. He won't know what hit him with two of us."

Warren smiled as he turned and walked to the shelf where the pottery was placed among the greenery and picked up a colorful piece. "Mom sure knows how to decorate a room, doesn't she? She even makes your desk look like it belongs."

I had to agree. It was decorated with the purpose of reflecting a room where a person could sit and contemplate and activate. In my mind it was the perfect office.

"It makes you feel really cool inside when you know you made a difference, doesn't it," Warren said quietly as he set the pottery back in its place. "I can't explain in words what I feel but I know why I feel it and it's cool." He looked at the computer screen, "I think your computer is warmed up now. Thanks Dad. See ya later."

As I watched him walk out through the door, I felt a part of me go with him, the part that doesn't ever want to let him go.

I thought of the courage Warren had shown when he found a way to earn money by baking and selling Mr. Britt's Cookies. Once again as I was a witness to that same courage. I had given him a little advice and he had taken that advice and put it into action. In doing so he had touched two lives, Anthony's and mine.

I finally turned to my computer and checked my e-mail and found, among the messages, an article entitled, *When You Thought I Wasn't Looking*. It caught my eye and I smiled as I read through the article. It listed all the things children learn by watching their parents. Its message; when you thought I wasn't looking, you taught me compassion, responsibility, to share, kindness, love, it's the little things that count, having trust in yourself, and knowing that it's ok to cry, was shared by an anonymous author. The last line summarized it all, *When you thought I wasn't looking, I looked at you and wanted to say, "Thanks for all the things I saw when you thought I wasn't looking."*

As I printed it out and set it aside for Joanna to read I decided to take the thought one step further. We teach our children even when we're not looking.

I knew of a young man who had been raised in a home where confusion and the lack of self-worth revealed the parent's inability to demonstrate love, learned anger, resentment and fear instead by watching the frustrations of his parents. At the age of fourteen, he was taken from the home and placed in foster care because of his aggressive behavior.

His foster parents brought order and stability into his life. Through their example he began to experience the feelings of trust and love.

By the time he was seventeen he had made remarkable changes. Love and self-worth replaced the anger that had been his driving force for so many years. He loved his life and he loved the family that had changed and reshaped it. His physical appearance took on the appearance of a confident young man, and he found purpose in his life. His foster family may not have known the impact of their example, but he had learned from them when they weren't looking.

When asked if he would like to return to his birth home, he quietly replied that though he loved his parents and siblings, he had no desire to return. His fear was that if he were placed back in that environment, he would once again become the person he had left behind.

At the age of eighteen, he graduated from high school with honors and received an excellent college scholarship. He now knew he had the power within himself to be anything he wanted to be if he took the responsibility to see it through. That knowledge gave him the ability to let go of the pain and anger he had harbored for so many years, and move on with his life.

I couldn't help but wonder what his future would have offered if he had remained in his birth home. Would he, with his anger unrestrained, have recognized his abilities? Maybe he would have, I don't know. The ability to do so was certainly within him but in that environment, would he have reached deep enough to find it? That is a question that cannot be answered since he chose to be removed from its influence, and, once again the law of 'cause and effect' had been in place.

It is true that we are molded by our experiences, by the presence or lack of love, and by what we see and hear. We are shaped by attitude as well as aptitude, and learn as we watch.

It is also true, however, that we alone decide how refined we will be in the end. This is a truth that cannot be disputed. The complexity of it is almost unique in its simplicity.

We have a choice of two directions in life. One is the road of self-centered, external gratification, and the other of simplicity and self-worth. The path of self-worth brings meaningful relationships, greater self-knowledge and a deeper connection to our own true nature and to the true nature of others. I believe the young man understood this concept because of his experiences, and he chose the path of self-worth.

One thing is certain. Everything that happens in our lives brings about change creating a different future for ourselves. It is our choice as to the future we create. It is within our power and, therefore, our responsibility to decide. We, in turn, teach when we are not looking.

Storing that idea in the back of my mind, I arrowed down and opened the next e-mail, it was a message reminding me of a conference meeting in Phoenix at 11:00 am, in two days. I hadn't forgotten the meeting, I just hadn't yet put together the information I needed so I spent the next hour organizing it and slipped it into the brief case before going in search of lunch.

There was a note on the cupboard from Joanna saying that she had taken Walker to the library to return the rest of the books they had been studying on snakes, and they would be back by 2:00 pm. Warren and Weston were visiting friends.

Will walked in just as I finished reading the note. "What's for lunch?" he asked as his removed his cap and tossed it on a chair.

"We're on our own today," I remarked as I scanned the contents of the fridge. "We can have whatever we want as long as it's in here and easy to make."

"Let's see who can make the best sandwich with what we find in here," he said, poking his head around the fridge door.

"Sounds like a good idea to me,"

"Where do you think ideas come from?" Will asked as we began creating our super sandwiches.

"I think the best ideas come from empty stomachs," I answered as I concentrated on how many items I could place on my sandwich and still fit it into my mouth. "Could you share a little of that mayo?" I watched him scrape the bottom of the jar, leaving it empty.

"Sorry, Dad, but to make a super sandwich you have to have this much mayo."

"Oh, I see." I heaved a hungry sigh as I found my way to the pantry for a new jar. I didn't know super sandwiches required so much mayo.

As I began piling on the cucumbers and tomatoes, adding sprouts and sliced avocado, Will added mustard, sesame seeds and onion to his turkey, lettuce, and tomatoes. As I covered mine with another slice of bread, he reached into the cupboard and found the peanut butter jar, opened the lid and scooped some out with a tablespoon.

"Tell me you are not going to add that to your sandwich," I pleaded.

"Of course not," he giggled, closing the jar, "the peanut butter's on the side. You just eat it by itself. It tastes better that way."

I didn't know that. I watched as he expertly separated a portion of the peanut butter on the tablespoon with his teeth and slid it into his mouth.

"Doesn't it get stuck to the roof of your mouth?"

"Yup."

"Doesn't that bother you?"

"Nope. You just suck it down."

I took his word for it and took two plates from the cupboard for our sandwiches. Will seemed to have forgotten all about the competition. It didn't matter, however, because he lost the minute he added black olive to his sandwich. I don't care for black olives.

"I think the best ideas come when you're all alone and no one can interrupt your brain," he said as he placed a slice of bread on top of the olives, then took a bite. Not allowing the need to chew interrupt the conversation, he continued. "I think our brain likes to think of ideas but our head gets so filled with other things, it won't let the brain think, and when the brain can't think it makes our head hurt and that's why we have headaches."

"That makes sense," I agreed. "Do you have a headache?"

"Yes, because my head is full of so much stuff."

"Are you all right?" I asked, a little concerned.

"Yup. Dad, how old do you have to be before people quit treating you so young?"

I looked at this little boy so full of questions and replied, "Let's see, you're eight now, how old do you think you should be before people stop treating you so young?"

"I think nine is a good age, don't you?"

"I think nine is the perfect age."

Before we could continue our conversation, Bella began barking and Will slid the rest of his peanut butter into his mouth, grabbed his sandwich, put his hat back on his head and said, "Gotta go now. Bella and I are going to play 'toss and fetch'," and off he ran, shouting to Bella that he was on his way.

I watched as the door closed behind him cutting off my view, and I began to feel the ache of loneliness in the silence of the kitchen, I watched him through the window as he picked up a stick and tossed it as far as his arm would allow him. I could hear his laughter as Bella ran, barking with excitement, to fetch it, and I missed his little boy questions and his little boy wisdom. In essence I was standing here, missing the little boy already that he would soon be leaving behind.

As I cleared away the lunch plates I made a mental note to add little boys to my list of miracles.

If I were to present the greatest seminar, I thought to myself, It would be nothing if when I came home there would be no one to greet me. No one to run to me and throw their arms around my neck. No one to look at me with the excitement of my return, in their eyes. I always love how Joanna greets me with a big hug and a kiss when I return home from traveling. Makes it all worth it. This is my success. What would my story be without them? It certainly would have very little meaning.

Seventeen years ago, I was locked into a self-centered state. I had worked my way through sadness and fear, to anger, and, finally, achieved self-centered pride, thinking I had everything I needed to make me happy and I didn't need help from anyone. I was completely satisfied taking care of myself.

I wonder what God's journal would reveal about me at that point in my life? I can only imagine...*Jim's pride seems to be getting in the way of his progress.*

Perhaps it is time to wake him from his dreary sleep.

Now, knowing the magnitude of the gift I had been given, I wonder if I have honored the rings I keep in the velvet box. Do I refer to their meanings and purpose as I raise my sons?

I have seen the qualities and truths the rings represent in each one of them as I watch them grow, and as I think back over the past seventeen years, I can see how these truths have helped to develop their lives.

I know in God's journal I would find an entry that would reiterate one basic principle. *Jim's children have given him an unwavering knowledge of me, and I am pleased.*

Before returning to my office, I looked out the window once again, and I could see Will and Bella, standing side by side, with their heads tipped upward, obviously looking at something in the sky. I heard Bella give a timid bark, then she was silent.

Just as I was turning to go into my office, I could see Weston out the other window. He had parked his bike and started walked toward Will, his eyes also looking upward.

My curiosity got the best of me and I changed directions. Work could wait this could not. I walked outside, lifted my head to the sky and with my hand shadowed my eyes from the sun. What I saw was breathtaking. A golden eagle, its wings in full span, was gracefully souring. I stood mesmerized as it lifted its wings to take it higher and then glide as it descended.

"Isn't it beautiful," Weston said as he came toward me. "Look at its wing span. Have you ever seen anything so incredible as an eagle in flight?"

"It is incredible, isn't it?" I replied.

We watched in silence for a few minutes then Weston explained, "Eagles are exceptional birds. They know a storm is coming long before it shows its face. They fly to a high spot and wait for the winds. When the storm hits, they are ready with their wings set so the wind will pick them up and lift them above the storm. Pretty cool, huh!"

"We could learn a lot from the eagle," I said as we watched the majestic bird land near the edge of our property.

"Do you think we could get a closer look?" Weston asked.

"If I can keep Bella here. You take Will, and the camera and see if you can get close enough for a picture. I'll make sure Bella stays."

Bella and I sat on my lounge chair as the two volunteers made their way toward the eagle.

The look in Bella's eyes told me she was not at all happy with this decision, but she was tolerating it. What she didn't realize was that I felt the same way. I just hope they have an opportunity to take some pictures.

"It's all right girl," I said, stroking her fur, "We shall ride out this storm together."

As I sat there consoling Bella I tried to imagine how it would feel to be an eagle, to spread my wings and capture the wind, then, let it lift me over the storm. It was a soothing thought.

We sat silently waiting for the boys to return for several minutes, then Bella raised her head and barked, and I knew they were on their way back, hopefully with some good pictures.

"Dad, Dad," I heard Will's voice as they appeared through the trees. "Guess what, Dad, we found the eagle. It was so cool."

"Great, did you get some pictures?"

"I zoomed in with the highest power on the lens and I think I got some really good shots," Weston said. "Through the zoom lens I could see its eyes. Do you know that eagles have really proud eyes?"

Before I could answer he continued, "Up close it looked powerful and fearless. Do you think eagles are ever afraid?"

"Only an eagle itself, can answer that question," I replied.

The next morning, as I was driving to the airport, I thought about the eagle and what it stands for. Does the eagle know something we don't know about being free?

There is a scripture that says, *"Then ye shall know the truth, and the truth shall make you free."* I think that scripture is talking not only about the spiritual self, but the total self as well. I don't think it is referring only to spiritual truths, but also temporal truths. How do we discover those truths? Maybe, instead of working so hard to try to understand what life is about or what God is about, or personal growth, or anything that isn't necessary in your life, you just need to understand that you are you. You are who you are right now, today. That's where the freedom comes in. You are free to be you. You are not the sum total of your experiences or current problems, but just you, with an imagination to create anything you want in life. The truth about who you are will set youn free.

The eagle understands this and he sours and glides and knows that he is an eagle. He stands majestic and proud of who he is, should we not do the same?

As I strapped myself into my seat on the plane, I couldn't help but feel a little bit of envy toward the eagle.

I had spent the first several minutes of the flight with my eyes closed and my mind opened, connecting with Baryon, my vital source of energy, I smiled wondering if sources of energy really do have imaginations. Weston had received an A+ on his story about energy, and some extra credit. His teacher had been so impressed she had read his story in faculty meeting the following Monday.

My mind was locked on little sources of energy running around with their heads full of imagination when I heard the flight attendant ask the young man in the seat next to me if he would like a drink. He ordered a tomato juice. Tomato juice sounded refreshing so I opened my eyes and ordered the same, and then glanced over to connect the face to the voice I had heard ordering the juice. He was well dressed in a conservative way, nothing out of the ordinary. But there was something about him that caught my eye. I could sense a strength of character in him that was unusually strong. I was curious and wanted to know more about him so I introduced myself. He smiled and did the same. We each explained our reason for being on the plane. He was a business executive for a firm in Phoenix and was on his way back from a business trip. I, in turn, was on my way to Phoenix for a business conference.

I had noticed a book in his hand. The title of the book was written in what appeared to be Russian. "Do you speak Russian?" I asked.

"I read it much better than I speak it," he explained. "This book, however, is actually written in Bulgarian. Even though they use the Russian alphabet, the Bulgarian language is somewhat different."

I asked him to translate the title into English, which he did, then he went on to explain that he had bought the book while living in Bulgaria several years ago and didn't want to lose his connection with the language, so whenever possible he would read one of several books he had brought back with him.

I was curious so I asked what had taken him to Bulgaria. He explained that he had volunteered his time, while in college, in a humanitarian effort to help the Bulgarian people make the transition from communism to the form of government they live under today.

"As I sat in the airport waiting for my flight to be called the day I left," he explained. "I was trying to envision what I was getting myself into. It wasn't until I had actually landed in Sofia, and found myself back in time at least thirty years that I began to realize the depth of my commitment. It was, in fact, the hardest thing I have ever done, and the most rewarding, for how else would I have grown and learned what I needed to know to make my own life more complete."

I became fascinated with the philosophy of this young man, and I asked him to explain in more detail how his time in Bulgaria had changed his life.

"I thought the cultural shock would be my greatest challenge," he spoke quietly, as if almost to himself, "but I was wrong. It was what I interpreted as a sense of hopelessness that consumed the hearts of the people. You could feel it as you spoke with them, you could see it in their eyes. I had never experienced anything like it before and I was unprepared. I knew if I was going to be successful in my humanitarian efforts I would have to reach inside and open my heart so it could feel what theirs felt."

He stopped talking for a moment and I could see his eyes begin to mist.

"As I stood in a bread line for the first time," he continued, holding back tears, "I tried to feel what I thought they were feeling, so I could understand. I wanted to experience the fear that lived inside every mother and father who stood there hoping to get enough bread for their children. I wanted to know for myself what it was like, but how could I grasp the meaning? Even though in order to eat that day, I had to stand and wait for whatever was being sold, I knew that I could walk away from it any time I wanted. These people could not for it was their life. I was foolish to think that I could understand?"

The flight attendant had returned with our juice so we had to stop our conversation long enough to pour the juice into the glasses. I wanted to learn more about this young man before our flight ended, and I had less than an hour. I didn't want to waste valuable time sipping juice so as soon as he had taken a drink, I asked him to tell me more.

"What I learned as I worked among these humble people," he said as he set his glass on the tray, "is that they have a strict devotion to their country. I witnessed an inner strength that seemed to contradict what I had felt in the food lines. In their tiny apartments, they displayed beautiful heirlooms, well preserved and honored. Delicate, hand crocheted doilies decorated worn couches and chairs. Colorful handmade trinkets relieved the reality of poverty. The people had made their homes a haven against oppression, and in their homes they became a free people. Hopelessness was a mask they wore only until they could close their doors against it.

They carried a deep sorrow in their hearts for their country as they watched it being desecrated by the government that controlled them, but as the rein of communism dissolved and the cloak of freedom embraced, the sorrow they had lived with for so long, dissipated, and their masks were removed.

I was impressed by the simplicity of their resourcefulness, the fierceness of their courage, and the strength of their love. It was my intent to teach and to help them, but, instead, they taught me, and now my life is more complete.

He stopped talking long enough to finish drinking his juice and then he asked, "Do you believe in God?"

I was startled by the question, It seemed out of character for him to ask, but I nodded that I did.

"What if you were told that you couldn't believe in God?"

"I can't comprehend it," I muttered.

"These people had been denied the opportunity to learn about God, and once he was introduced into their lives they could not quench their hunger for the knowledge of Him and they became like sponges, absorbing whatever they could read and hear concerning God. With that knowledge came a joy they had never felt before and they were truly free.

The stewardess announced that we would be landing in five minutes. I didn't want the conversation to end but I only had time to thank the man for sharing his story with me and wish him well in his future, knowing he had a successful one ahead of him.

As I made my way to the rental car service, I thought how ironic it was that in the past two days I had seen freedom in the eagles' wings and had heard freedom in a young man's heart, and I knew I had gathered more insight into my definition of the word freedom, and I, too, was more complete because of this experience.

Freedom is not given or taken away. Freedom is what we make of it. People who live under oppression, yet still maintain their freedom are actually more free than people who have freedom, but still live in the state of oppression. Freedom is a personal choice.

The meeting had been both successful and brief, and I had a few minutes at the airport before catching the plane. Sometimes I feel like I'm revolving in de'ja'vu. It was a quiet day at the airport so I leaned back in my seat, closed my eyes and let pleasant memories flow.

I have come a long way in the past seventeen years, in discovering who I am. Many people have influenced my life. People I've met in my seminars and people I've met in airports, like C.T., the artist who gave me deeper insight into faces, and the sweet and profound 80-year old woman with the lovely white hair, who advised me to go out and make someone's day.

I think living in a trailer taught me that it doesn't matter how close the space but how close the love.

I've learned to accept the sweetness of death and to realize death is really life beyond a veil that can be parted when love provides the way.

I've learned to appreciate the silent rhythm of the rain and the melody of nature. I have found that there is hope in hopelessness and responsibility in freedom.

I know that wisdom comes in the giving and that grandmas should make the rules, and, more importantly, that being a good mom is a job far beyond the ability of a man.

I have seen the miracle of daffodils in bloom, and angels in the tree through the eyes of a child, and I understand them better. I have witnessed the faith of a child, and I now have more faith, not only in God, but also in myself.

The story of "Alice in Wonderland," now has new meaning to me, and I'm thankful for the path I choose that has led me to this day.

I have found that a house is just a house, no matter the size, until it is filled with things that matter most that make it a home, and that almonds taste so much better when they are offered from the hand of a little boy.

There are times I thought I would like to revisit the past. Not to change anything, nor would I want to, but to better understand the motivation. Maybe, in a spiritual sense, over the past several months, I have done just that. Something that seems to remain a mystery to me, however, is how my journal found its place to my desk that day, and started me on this journey of rediscovery.

As I boarded the plane, I felt suddenly very homesick and I knew that having family is the greatest accomplishment I will ever achieve for they are my life, my messengers of truth.

During the flight home I felt a deep longing and I recognized it as a longing for home. As I drove onto my newly paved driveway, I saw Joanna standing in the doorway to greet me, and I knew I was home.

"It seems like we do a lot of this saying 'hello' and 'goodbye' thing," she said softly. "I've missed you and you've only been gone one day." She gave me a big hug and a soft kiss, which a so appreciated.

I understood her feeling. I had missed home as if I had been gone forever, and, I found myself searching for ways to solve the feeling for both of us. If I could limit my travel or call her more often, or take her with me on more occasions. Then it occurred to me, instead of trying to think of ways to change my own patterns of work, I should simply be experiencing the feeling of being loved enough by this beautiful woman to be missed. What an appropriate homecoming I had just received.

It wasn't late yet so I invited Joanna to take a walk with me. The moon was just making its entrance bringing with it the four stars I had given her several weeks ago. We held hands as we walked slowly in the direction of the oak tree and watched them grow in their brilliance.

"Have you ever wondered what it would be like," I asked, "to walk through the rainforests of Peru?"

"Not really?" she answered, looking at me as if she were trying to access the validity of the question. "Why do you ask?"

"I've been invited to do a spiritual retreat in Peru."

"And?"

"And I was thinking that it might be a great opportunity to take my discoveries to the next level."

"Let's hug an oak tree instead," Joanna said as we approached its limbs, so, while still holding each other's hand we wrapped our arms around the trunk and hugged tightly while Joanna giggled and I laughed. The trunk felt warm and friendly in the coolness of the night and it graciously shared its happiness with us.

"Did you know," I said, "that some tree huggers are self-conscience and after they hug a tree they look around to see if anyone was watching?"

"Really," Joanna gave me an unbelieving look from behind the trunk of the tree.

"Yes, and did you know that when they do that, it spoils the moment. People are already thinking whatever they are thinking about them anyway, so when you hug a tree, you've got to just hug a tree and enjoy it."

"Can we stay out and play for a while?" Joanna asked, innocently, "All the dishes are done." "Ok, but I have to be home by midnight," I replied and I picked a small wild flower and weaved it into her hair. I found my favorite spot and sat, leaning my back against the huge trunk of the oak. Joanna found her favorite spot and sat, leaning her back against me. I wrapped my arms around her and held her close, and we watched our stars, and they winked back at us.

Would we be out here, under this oak tree, watching the stars if I had been home all day? I don't know but I have just figured out that so often our need to fix the problem, or rescue someone from their feelings, keeps us from experiencing the love and tenderness at hand. Most often intimacy arises not from an attempt to take away or heal the pain, but living through it together, instead. Not from trying to work it out, but from being with it. Love, trust and intimacy deepens from holding and being held, both physical as well as emotionally.

As I held Joanna close in a welcomed embrace, I could see, in my mind, the painting of intimacy I had painted for her, hanging on the wall, and I knew I had just discovered another meaning of the word intimacy that blended right into the painting without disturbing it.

"Have you set a date for your trip?" Joanna smiled as she wrapped her fingers through mine.

"I've been waiting to talk to you first," I said quietly, not to disturb the mood.

"I think you should go if that is what you need to do." She lifted my hand to her lips and gently kissed it.

"Do you know what I think?" I asked

"Sometimes," she replied,

"Do you know what I'm thinking right now?"

"What you are thinking right now?"

"I think the strength of love awaits us in the receiving, not in the negotiating. I think the strength of love is in accepting each other and not trying to problem solve each other. I think the strength lies in the listening and affirmation, not in trying to change or fix those we love and care deeply about. But most of all, I think you already knew that, while I am just beginning to learn."

"Do you know what I think?" Joanna asked

"Sometimes," I replied.

"Do you know what I'm thinking right now?"

"What are you thinking right now?"

"I think you already knew that too. I think you just needed to put it into words we both could understand." She snuggled a little closer and then whispered, "Do you ever see the angels in the tree."

I held her a little tighter and whispered back, "I see angels every day, they are my messengers of truth."

Reflections

Journal Entry

What brings us to the moment of our life when we know we have found contentment? I don't mean that we have found a way to eliminate all of our problems, but a way to make the best of life in spite of them. When do we reach that point?

> *If I can touch another's life,*
> *Through something I have done.*
> *If I can make a difference,*
> *In the life of just that one,*
> *Then I am content.*

WHAT I HAVE LEARNED FROM MY SIX SONS

If I can let ideas come,
When my brain is free.
And any time I care to,
I can go and hug a tree
Then I am content.

I am content with the fact that natural laws are constant and cannot be changed with a signature on a piece of paper.

It's a fact that if you don't want something to happen,
The best way to insure it doesn't happen,
Is to make sure the condition that would cause to event
Never takes place.

It's a fact that life is what you make it
You give it all you've got,
Or you give it nothing,
And life returns the favor.

It's a fact that if your wife decorates your office,
Everything in that office
Will be the reflection
Of what she thinks of you.

It's a fact that everything in our life brings change,
We decide to move forward or backward,
It is our choice, therefore, our responsibility,
For we teach when we are not looking.

I think it is good to have a father/son lunch. It's important to know how much mayo it takes to make a super sandwich, and that peanut butter is better when eaten from a spoon.

The dog's bark,
Called him out to race.
Though I heard his laughter
I could not see his face.

The room no longer held
The sound of his voice
Full of little boy questions
Of a little boy's choice.

My heart longed for,
A little boy's embrace
The joy in his eyes
The smile on his face

In the innocence of their smiles, children unveil a power that captures the heart and nurtures the soul. With that power they can sour above the storm and they are free. If we could hang onto that innocence, would we be as powerful as the eagle in flight?

An eagle in flight is the breath of freedom.
There is power is his wings.
As he captures the wind,
And glides above the storm.

A man's freedom is not given or taken away,
For it is what he makes of it.
If there is freedom in his heart
He has made the choice.

Joanna told me that Will and I are very much alike because we are always thinking. I think I'll write down what I am thinking.

I think hugging a tree with someone you love is the best way to hug a tree.
I think love is the greatest of all miracles.
I think the strength of love awaits us in the receiving and the accepting.
I think the strength of love lies in the listening and affirmation.
I think I see angels every day because love surrounds me.

Thought for Today

Lift your thoughts as high as the eagle lifts its wings
So they may sour above the storm
For what we believe, we are

Epilogue

There are some things in our lives we have to accept on faith because man's knowledge does not contain enough facts to comprise all truths. That's why we have imaginations.

The poet, John Masefield, wrote, *"Man consists of body, mind and imagination. His body is faulty, his mind untrustworthy, but his imagination has made him remarkable."*

John F. Kennedy said in a statement, *"The problems of the world cannot possibly be solved by skeptics or cynics whose horizons are limited by the obvious realities. We need men who can dream of things that never were."*

What happens to limit our horizons? How do we begin to dream of things that never were?

Education, background or experience do not limit our horizons, insight does that for us. We have to penetrate the barrier that clogs our inner vision and surrender the part of us that blinds our heart and soul.

It takes courage to let go of the familiar you, to move to the next level of discovery, because every life level requires a different you. We need to check our ego in at the door and enter the room, teachable.

Without the ego, "which is all our past experiences, programming and beliefs," we become resourceful, our vision begins to clear, and we are not afraid to allow others to see who we really are. We accept ourselves and we accept others. Our hearts are open to compassion. We are able to give ourselves, in full, to commitment and appreciate what we receive in return.

If we can accept that life is a miracle, then harmony and balance become a part of our universe. We become responsible which empowers us with freedom. Freedom and responsibility are inseparable. Freedom is the nature of the universe. It is with our freedom we learn to create. To create, there has to be a purpose. The purpose is love.

Just as in the universe where all things have to have order, so it is in life, once all these things are in order, our imaginations are boundless for our minds, hearts, and spirits are free.

As I have read my journal entries, I have watched my truths become clearer in content as well as vision. I know, through my own experiences, that children are, by nature, spiritual. They have a natural acceptance of the purpose of life until we come along and infiltrate that purity with fears, doubts and our own insecurities. We begin to distort their picture of life and limit their creativity and imaginations because our own are limited.

We just want to be happy, but life keeps getting in the way. We don't realize that happiness is life. We should treasure every moment we are alive. When you spend a minute, you have one less minute to spend. Time waits for no one. It ruthlessly passes us by. There is so much out there for us to create and to discover, we just need to empty our minds of all the stuff that makes our heads hurt so our imaginations can gain access into our minds.

I read somewhere that *"God has not given us the spirit of fear, but of power and of love and of a sound mind to overcome it." Fear is a made up story. It is proof of our ability to create.*

I believe we have a responsibility to follow through with our end of the bargain in using what has been given us.

All these thoughts come to my mind as I prepare to leave for Sedona to present a workshop and spiritual retreat. I also had an invitation to bring my retreat to Peru, which is the opportunity to venture into the rainforests and be introduced to one of the ancient tribes that live deep within its confines. In doing my research, I recognize the dangers involved in this journey to the little known regions of Peru, yet I feel a deep desire to discover for myself what exists there.

I haven't forgotten the words of the young man on the plane when he said, "It was the hardest thing I have ever done and yet the most rewarding, for how else would I have grown and discovered what I needed to know to make my own life more complete."

The words, *How else could I have grown*...continue to echo in my mind, and I wonder why those words stir me so? They are familiar, yet I can't place them.

I closed my eyes to meditate and slowly I began to recall words Alea had spoken to me long ago, "*I am here to honor your growth...Get out of your own way...enjoy the journey.*"

Alea could do nothing for me. The discovery of the truths was my own choosing. The decision was, and always has been, up to me. Yet I knew it was her influence that guided me. Now, I just have to get out of my own way and get on with the journey.

In my deepest imagination, I realize that I will be moving to the next level of discovery as I step into my retreat and once again become the student. There are still many things I need to learn that will expand my creativity, heighten my spirituality and make my life more complete. With my fascination of a possible Peru trip, I wonder, could it be Alea's influence that draws me there?

What I'll find once I arrive, I don't know. I remember the day, however, that Alea had placed her hand on my heart and said, *"Trust yourself. Be resourceful and know that you are loved. We shall meet again, someday."*

My soul is quickened at the thought, and I feel an excitement I am at a loss to explain.

To be continued...

Thought for Today

If you do what you do with love,
you'll have only what you love in your life.

About Jim Britt

Jim Britt is an internationally recognized leader in the field of peak performance and personal empowerment training. He is author of 13 best-selling books, including *Rings of Truth; Cracking the Rich Code; The Power of Letting Go; Freedom; Unleashing Your Authentic Power; Do This. Get Rich-For Entrepreneurs; The Flaw in The Law of Attraction;* and *The Law of Realization,* to name a few.

Jim is also the co-creator and co-author of *"The Change"* collaborative book series that is published and distributed worldwide.

Jim has presented seminars throughout the world sharing his success principles and life-enhancing realizations with thousands of audiences, totaling over 1,500,000 people from all walks of life.

Jim has served as a success counselor to over 300 corporations worldwide. He was recently named as one of the world's top 20 success coaches and presented with the best of the best award out of the top 100 contributors of all time to the direct selling industry. He was the late great Jim Rohn's business partner for almost 10 years where Tony Robbins worked under his direction for his first five years in the speaking business.

Jim is more than aware of the challenges we all face in making adaptive changes for a sustainable future.

To Schedule Jim Britt as your featured speaker at your next convention or special event, or to host a workshop, email: JimBritt@jimbritt.com

For more information on Jim visit his website at www.JimBritt.com or to purchase the prequel "Rings of Truth" and other programs offered.

"Master your moment as they become hours that become days.
Your legacy awaits."

Jim Britt

www.ingramcontent.com/pod-product-compliance
Lightning Source LLC
Chambersburg PA
CBHW070053080526
44586CB00013B/1031